T0196226

Under, In, and Outside the Box

Teaching ALL of the Children

B A R B A R A   B A R B E R

authorHOUSE®

AuthorHouse™
1663 Liberty Drive
Bloomington, IN 47403
www.authorhouse.com
Phone: 1-800-839-8640

First published by AuthorHouse 7/21/2011

ISBN: 978-1-4634-3463-2 (e)
ISBN: 978-1-4634-3462-5 (sc)

Printed in the United States of America

Any people depicted in stock imagery provided by Thinkstock are models, and such images are being used for illustrative purposes only. Certain stock imagery © Thinkstock.

This book is printed on acid-free paper.

Dedication

This book is for you, Brittany, my beautiful granddaughter, and for anyone else in college learning to be a teacher. I hope the stories will help you be a great Teacher. You will notice I capitalized Teacher. What it takes to be a Teacher is to look at each child who has a behavior or handicap that is preventing him from succeeding, and figuring out what you can do. To do this, I've discovered over 40 years of working with children with regular and special needs that we have to use creativity, experience, determination, and love. There is never a single, sure way to accomplish the change necessary for the student's success.

Being creative is difficult, especially when you may be surrounded by teachers of the lower-case "t" persuasion, and you definitely will be! Being creative is showing that you are unafraid to try crazy, bizarre, off-the-wall ideas that may require a ton of effort on your part. Being creative is being brave. Being creative can cost you time and money. Being creative can fail many times but then, suddenly it all works and you have success!

Using your experience doesn't just mean your experience as a Teacher; it also means using the experience of other Teachers. Don't be afraid to ask, to observe, to read, to write to others, or to go to the Internet. As your own experience builds, remember all the different students and all the different attempts and successes that are helping you build your toolbox. I guarantee you, though, that even after many years of teaching, you will meet a child who will need a unique solution. Why? He will be an individual with his own set of experiences and problems and he will need a new creative solution.

Determination and perseverance are the characteristics every good Teacher needs in order to win. Always **know** you will solve the riddle and figure out what will work to change a child destined for failure into a child who will revel in success. When one try after the next fails, your determination will cause you to rethink your plan, to change your methods, to try and try and try again until you succeed. Persevere and you will win.

Does "love" have to be explained here? I think so because I have heard many, many times that you must stay completely objective as a Teacher. I say "Nonsense." You certainly need to be a Teacher, not a mother, not a father, but a Teacher, but does that mean a lack of love? No, not if you understand my definition of the love of a Teacher. Love means a Teacher looks at a dirty or naughty or foul-mouthed or shy or irritating or rock-throwing or kicking or hitting or loud or obnoxious or physically handicapped, or mentally handicapped, or emotionally handicapped, or uncooperative child and is *positively* sure that he would rather be a clean, well behaved, sweet talking, outgoing, fun-to-be-around, kind-to-other-children, sweet-natured child who is able to get where he wants to go, to learn what he needs for success, and is well balanced enough to become a self-supporting, tax-paying, happy adult. That's love, especially if you are being kicked, bitten, or hit while you are thinking these thoughts!

This book is filled with stories of real children although the names have been changed. All of the stories are true because I lived them, and I hope they demonstrate the positive attitude you'll be able to put into your toolbox to help you be a Teacher, one of those with a capital "T."

Introduction

I'm a Teacher. I'm capitalizing Teacher because I earned that after 40 successful years in the profession. I've been retired for a few years and now that I can really reflect on so many students, classes, and situations I see I have something I can give back to the profession. My grandmother was an elementary teacher, and now my granddaughter is beginning her freshman year in college with hopes of becoming a teacher. It seems to be a family affair. I'd love to be able to put my 40 years of failures and successes into her head, but I know that isn't possible, so I've dedicated this book to her and all the education students who might benefit.

When I went through my college training I never dealt with a single child until I did my student teaching at the end of my program. Times have mercifully changed for education students. I student- taught in sixth grade, and I was planning to teach awhile before getting a Master's in Special Education. The class was huge but well controlled when the actual teacher was in the room. The second he left, though, butterflies swarmed through my stomach and the rowdies got rowdier. I learned a lot by the end of the semester, but one piece of advice stood out and I never forgot it. My cooperating teacher noticed that I had tried to get control by listing names of those who disrupted while he was out of the room. He told me, "If you are going to put a kid's name up in lights, make it for something good." Wow! So simple, and so wonderfully true.

My first teaching year was 1964. I was 21 years old. Again I taught sixth grade, this time in a new school. I had 44 students. We were unbelievably overcrowded and I was incredibly overwhelmed. I tried so hard, too hard, to make all the textbooks come out even by the end of the school year, but it was hopeless. Some students were weak in skills needed to even begin where sixth grade starts.

I had a boy in the class who was extremely hyperactive, couldn't stay seated, and was overly stimulated by everything. I had no training in knowing what to do and he stymied me. One day I pulled down the wall map of the world and he rushed up and started naming countries all over the map, so excited he couldn't even stand still to do it. He hopped up and down, "Here's England! I went to England!"

One of my other boys that year was constantly in trouble with the police. He stole, vandalized homes, and broke curfew. We had a meeting about him and I discovered his mom was a juvenile parole officer and his dad was a police officer. They were recently divorced. I used to say he was fitting in as a juvenile delinquent. That wasn't very nice, though.

This was the second lesson that lasted my whole career. Get to know the families of your students. I made home visits starting with my second year of teaching and continued it throughout my career. When you read the stories in the book, you'll realize how important those home visits were to my success. It is truly critical to know what the student's life is all about, not just how he does from 8:30 to 3:00.

After I got my Master's in Special Education, I began 35 years working with children with disabilities. My classrooms, until 1996, were designated for moderately mentally handicapped children, those who used to be called *Trainable Mentally Handicapped* children. I taught in segregated schools in which all of the students were mentally handicapped, and self-contained classrooms in regular elementary schools. I taught in fully integrated classrooms in regular elementary schools. I taught in reverse mainstreaming preschool programs (a mixture of regular and special ed students) and taught all ages from three to 22. After retiring in 1996 and moving to a small town, I was hired as a consultant for special education departments in several area schools, primarily mentoring teachers and aides, setting up programs and providing strategies for staff. The stories in this book highlight children from all of those years.

For over 10 years, I tutored children in the evenings and in the summer. I tutored all ages, most subjects, and all types of students including gifted children, mentally handicapped children, high school-aged children having difficulty with a single subject, and elementary regular ed students who were struggling with math, reading, or writing. It was amazing what I learned during those 10 years. The children succeeded because they knew I liked them, admired them, was proud of them, and would never put them down. They weren't afraid to try, even if they failed. Because they weren't afraid to try, they did try, and eventually, they did learn!

Perhaps the saddest part of the teaching profession is the burnout rate. After only a handful of years, many teachers go into other careers. I think the most important way to avoid that is to laugh. Have a sense of humor and talk with fellow teachers and let yourself enjoy a great big laugh about whatever is going on. Humor will get you through just about any situation.

At the end of the day, what were the most important lessons I learned during my long career? I'd say that success in teaching is demonstrated by how a student feels about himself and how a student demonstrates self-confidence. It isn't so much what we've taught him, but how he has made it his own and how he uses it. I learned that ridicule and sarcasm will kill the likelihood of any self-confidence occurring and they have absolutely **no** place in education. I learned that parents knew their children far better than I ever could, but I could guide them to help their children. And I learned that no book can make you a successful Teacher. Books, like this one, can give you ideas, but you have to possess the key ingredients yourself. You must truly like children and their habits, you must treat each child as an individual, you must listen to children and parents, and you must believe, with your entire heart and being that you will succeed with **every** child.

Acknowledgements

Many of my fellow teachers and parents of my students have encouraged me to write a book about my positive educational philosophy. I have finally accomplished the task and hope the stories of these 25 children express my love of teaching and my desire to share what I have learned through the years. I appreciate all of the parents and teachers who helped me reach this point.

My cousin, Melvin Young, was a boy with Downs Syndrome. There were no educational opportunities at all for him in his life. He was 3 years younger than I and fascinated me. My desire to teach special education was a direct result of my concern for my cousin and his lack of opportunity. I thank him for that inspiration because I have loved my career.

My family enjoyed my teaching stories for the duration of my career and always assumed I would write this book. The final catalyst was my granddaughter who decided to follow her dream to become a teacher. My goal is to help her know that a positive attitude is the key to success with children. By reading about these children, I hope she will appreciate each child she meets during her future career.

Primarily, I thank all of the children I taught during my 41 year career. I chose 25 children but there were several hundred other stories I could have told. Each child taught me a great deal, and I thank them for being in my life.

Table of Contents

important part each plays for several years demonstrates the continued involvement of a trusted teacher in the parent-child dynamic through the school years.

Chapter 7: Donald 45

A highly verbal kindergarten boy is handicapped not only by mental retardation, but by a severe learning disability at the labeling level of learning. This chapter suggests unusual techniques to use association to break through the difficulty of labels. It also discusses the critical importance of discovering the best learning style for each student.

Chapter 8: Frank 51

An elementary boy with cerebral palsy experiences the joy of self-propulsion in an electric wheelchair and the staff learns valuable lessons from him and his mother. His story reiterates the importance of educating all students to be the most independent adults they can possibly be.

Chapter 9: James 55

This is the tragic story of a neglected, unloved, unlovable child who changes when he is listened to and talked to with kindness and consideration. It is a lesson in never considering a child to be hopeless and in how to alter a child's environment to help him succeed.

Chapter 10: Jason 61

A fifth grade boy with Down's Syndrome wanted to be a violinist. His story which demonstrates the power of motivation and self-determination.

Chapter 11: Tommy 65

This chapter relates the remarkable journey of a non-verbal, aggressive fourth grade boy who began to improve when he was befriended by a fourth grade peer. It focuses on the acceptance of every child and the importance of promoting a sense of community and safety in the classroom.

explain how to move from the inappropriate, but temporarily necessary reward, to the more appropriate, intrinsic reward.

Chapter 24: Nancy 127

Nancy was a non-verbal girl with cerebral palsy. She was violent and very strong. This chapter tells the results of the attempts to help her become an appropriate student. It is a chapter emphasizing the need for extra aide support with some students and also the need for cooperation from the district authorities.

Chapter 25: Barry 133

This chapter is about a boy from age 7 to 12 who was in a special education classroom. It is the story of a wild, undisciplined, aggressive, hyperactive second grader who eventually became a delightful 7th grader. The process of civilizing Barry demonstrates the importance of patience, the power of believing all children deserve the best we have to offer, and the need to develop the best classroom climate to enable learning to take place.

Chapter 1:

Jimmy

On Back-to-School night a young mom came in with her two really little girls clutching her hands. Suddenly, she looked back for her son who had stayed in the hall. I glanced up and saw an adorable chubby, bright-eyed face peeking around the door frame into his new world. There was no smile, though, and then, there was no face! Mom let go of the girls and rushed back out into the hall and the chase was on.

It only took a couple of seconds of looking at that impish face and I knew Jimmy would be one of my favorites. I was teaching a class of moderately mentally delayed intermediate-aged students. This boy had Downs Syndrome, he had no language, he was overweight, and he obviously loved his mom a lot. He preferred the summer lifestyle: sleep 'til you wake up, eat whatever you want, whenever you want, lie on the floor and look at magazines, go eat whatever you want, whenever you want, watch cartoons and laugh, laugh, laugh, eat whatever you want, whenever you want, go outside and make your sisters get out of the swings and then swing and swing and swing and then go eat lunch. That sums up Jimmy. He was spoiled just a bit.

The year Jimmy started in my class was my first year of teaching my students in a total integration model with two fifth grade classes, half my students in each class. The teachers of the two classes team taught and now we would be a team of three with 70 students altogether, 35 in each room. We had had a partial integration program the year before to see where the "bugs" might be. Our goal was to be completely integrated but meet all of the needs of each group of students. Jimmy needed to learn to communicate, to care for his basic needs, and to become as independent and socially acceptable as possible.

When I met with his mother to set up his goals she couldn't imagine that her son could ever learn a fraction of what I suggested, but she went along with my ideas. She also worried very much that he would be lost in the crowd of 70 students. It may sound unbelievable, but our program was very well organized. Since there were three teachers involved, we had three adjacent classrooms. All of the academic work was done in two classrooms and we used the third classroom for times when we combined all of the students.

Once a week my class spent the entire day in the community learning functional life skills. We had units on skating, hiking, swimming, park activities, bowling, and so on. We went out for lunch each week to learn to order, to use good manners in restaurants, and to use money. We also went grocery shopping. Each student had a list of four items and the money in his wallet to pay for them. One regular education student from each of the two classes had the opportunity to go with us by turning in all his or her homework for that week.

Jimmy started the year wanting only to do his own thing. During any group activity, he sat and held any object he could find and watched it while he made it sway back and forth. He didn't listen at all when we were in a group. If he were called on, he put his head down or turned around and put his back to the teacher. He did like his desk, though. When he was supposed to be somewhere else, like in a math lesson, for example, he would constantly run back to his desk. He never said any words at all. He didn't need to, at least as far as he was concerned. I didn't agree.

When each morning began, the fifth graders were given something they had to do the minute they sat down: a math problem, a sentence to correct, or something to read. It was a way to set the tone immediately. My students, who were scattered around the room, one in each cluster of 6 desks, had their sticker cards, used to reinforce good behavior, and schedules on their desks, and their job was to write their names on each.

Jimmy was unable to write his name and he didn't trace. He had no interest in it. His card and schedule had his first name printed with a highlighter, to encourage him to trace it, but initially my goal was for him to pick up the pencil and try, which he stubbornly refused to do. Kyle, who sat next to Jimmy, became fascinated by him and made it his job to be sure Jimmy learned to write his name. I held Jimmy's hand with the pencil and traced his name with him for the first couple of days and then Kyle said to me, "Mrs. Barber, I can help Jimmy." At first, as Kyle helped him, Jimmy giggled, but from that moment on, Jimmy's progress was amazing. I've always noticed that a child learns best from another child and this case proved it again. By October, Jimmy was picking up his pencil and trying hard to trace, with Kyle's encouragement. Kyle would say, "Write your name, Jimmy, while I do my work" and Jimmy would pick that pencil up and scribble on his name. By November, Kyle decided that wasn't good enough and he literally insisted that Jimmy "follow the line" and amazingly, Jimmy tried; by December he could trace his first name.

What impressed me so much was how matter-of-fact Kyle was about Jimmy's abilities. He knew Jimmy could do it, and he did it. By the end of that first school year, Kyle had made a greater difference in Jimmy than anyone could have imagined. He began saying single words at Kyle's insistence and he wanted to play with Kyle on the playground.

That didn't always happen, but Kyle never rejected him. By February, Jimmy was printing his first name, which we shortened to Jim, by using his pencil while following someone's finger. We didn't have to touch him, or hold his hand, and he could produce "Jim". By the end of the year, he could print his name if told the letters, but he often made only one hump on the "m". Kyle made it his business each morning to be sure Jimmy made that "m" correctly.

At the beginning of the next school year, we were in our second year of the integration experiment, but now our old fifth grade friends had moved on and were sixth graders. By October, Jimmy was able to print "Jim" independently. Soon after, Kyle, now a sixth grader, came to visit us and asked how Jim was doing. We said he was great, but Kyle said, very seriously, "No, I mean with his name. Is he making two humps on that 'm'?"

That kind of dedication from Kyle during the previous year is the reason I could say, "Absolutely *yes.*" Kyle beamed.

We had a sharing time with the fifth graders in our schedule that first year. The teacher would ask for volunteers, and many of my students participated very well, but not Jimmy. He was happy and content to sit with the group on the floor, but he didn't seem to listen and he definitely didn't participate. When we called on him and asked him to stand up, he just turned away from us and rocked back and forth. We made some progress but mostly it was just getting him to stay seated facing the same direction as the others.

By February, Jimmy felt very comfortable with the fifth graders and the routine, and he started to be a little silly. That was good because it was a form of social interaction, even though he found humor at inappropriate times. The other kids realized that he loved to "high 5" so that became Jimmy's way of striking up relationships. On Valentine's Day he brought valentines for each of the students and as he passed them out, he high 5'd each student who loved it. He started becoming quite popular. Even though his giggling and his constant high fives could be a distraction, they were actually solving one of his big problems, a lack of social interaction. Soon, during the sharing time, we began to see that Jim kept his head up and he started paying attention to the children who spoke, but he still refused to stand up or say anything. Toward the end of the school year, a student had brought an article from the newspaper about a drug bust at one of the local high schools. Mrs. McNulty, my team teacher, suddenly looked at Jim and said, "Is it good to take drugs?" and he said, "NO!" We all nearly fainted. One word and we were almost in tears. All the children clapped. He grinned from ear to ear, aware of his success.

The second year we changed this sharing time to a current events time, and students brought in an article from a newspaper to share. The kids sat on the floor and the child who was sharing stood next to the teacher. Jimmy no longer turned away; he watched each child, but he rarely participated. More and more often we were able to get him to repeat a key word from their article. In October, this is what I wrote in my parent newsletter:

> *"The biggest event of this week (and maybe this year) was that during Current Events one day this week Mrs.McNulty asked the students, "Does anyone have a current event article to share?" Jimmy (yes, the same boy who spent all of last year ignoring us when called on) RAISED HIS HAND up high, totally unprompted, and when Mrs. McNulty called on him, he STOOD UP, walked to the front, held up his article about the Phoenix Suns, and said, "Ball" Mrs. McNulty, my aide, Cynthia, and I were speechless. We were just speechless. Can you believe it? That's the power of patience!"*

At the home visit with Jimmy's mom at the start of the first year, she had talked about how difficult it was for her to go anywhere with him. He was frightened in crowds, ran from her in the grocery store, and didn't want to share with his sisters. When I told her that we would be having swimming lessons once a week all year, she told me he was terrified of the water and she couldn't imagine any way on earth that we would get him in the pool. I assured her we would. She didn't believe it. When I told her we would be teaching him to skate, she laughed. Everything about Jimmy was round, including his feet, so it was a little hard to imagine how we would find skates to fit, but we knew we would. Home visits are fantastic and so very helpful. It's important to know what the parents' concerns, fears, and hopes are. Many times I discovered, as in Jim's case, that my expectations were quite a bit higher for the child than those of his parents.

Let's start with swimming. Jimmy was willing to walk around in the very shallow end, but he wouldn't go near deeper water. If forced, he screamed loudly and got a grip on your neck and had to be pried off. For the first few weeks, we developed the routine of getting him in the suit, getting him in the shallow end, and then we let him sit on his towel near the deep end (about 15 feet away). Amazingly, by the end of October that first year, he actually was willing to sit on the decking at the side of the deep end of the pool. Our first major breakthrough came in November when he willingly gave up the death grip and held a kick board with both hands while I held him up with my hand on his stomach. He kicked and seemed to enjoy it. We were so happy. By the end of January, once we pried his hands from around my neck, we were able to give him a push start and he paddled about 10 feet to the side of the pool. At the end of the first year, he could paddle the width of the pool which was about 20 feet. His mom was totally amazed and even came to watch because I don't think she could believe it. He was still scared of the deep water, though.

The second year was incredible. During the summer, his mom had been able to go to the pool with her children, including Jimmy, and he had not lost any of the skills he had learned the year before. By October we started forcing him to jump in at the deep end (about 5 feet deep) but we held his hand and someone was in the water to be right with him to give him a push to start him toward the side. In December, I wrote this in my newsletter to parents:

> *"Our student of the week is Jim. We had just about one of the most exciting days Thursday at the pool. He jumped **independently** into the deep end of the pool. Not only once but three times! I could tell you of the many days we've spent with him screaming in that pool. Wow! What a great, wonderful Christmas present Jim gave us."*

Jimmy loved to eat, so going out to eat once a week was a favorite time for him. We had goals for each student and spent about six weeks in each restaurant. Some fast food restaurants required getting in a "first available cashier" line, some had individual lines behind each cash register, some gave numbers, and some made the drinks, and in some you filled your own cups- lots to learn. The first time we went, Jimmy couldn't carry a tray with a drink on it without spilling, but by the end of that semester, he was a pro. He could say "Happy Meal" at McDonald's and that seemed to work for him anywhere they served Kids Meals. In the "sit-down" restaurants, we taught the students to order from a menu, leave the items on the table (sugar, silverware, etc.) alone before the food arrived, and to understand to put their napkins in their laps. We practiced in the classroom and then once in the restaurant, the student got what he ordered. The first week, Jimmy refused to order, so he didn't eat. That didn't happen again! In the sit down restaurant our rule was that any student who remembered to put the napkin in his lap, would get ice cream for dessert. We started this in January and by April, Jimmy got ice cream and he knew exactly why.

For most of the previous weeks, we had to remind him and then he played with the napkin too much. He also played with the silverware, which we worked on all that first year.

The second year we started with fast food and he was quite proficient. He could carry the tray with the food and drink on it and always ordered. One day, he just said "Coke" and I thought that was going to be all he had, but the cashier asked, "Anything else?" and he said "Happy Meal" so he was fine. Once we started going to the sit down restaurants in January, he quickly remembered about the napkin-in-the-lap -equaling ice cream for dessert and by our third week, he was getting the ice cream each time. Once he got that trick down pat, I added leaving the silverware alone until the food came as a condition for ice cream, but that was almost instantly successful.

The first week we went grocery shopping, we realized Jimmy was a wild man with the cart. Most of my students had no experience pushing a grocery cart when they started in the class, and after an end display went down, I was sure that was the case with Jim. He was fascinated with his "wheels" and went way too fast. For several weeks, our goal for him was for him to push the cart successfully up and down the aisles and then we would take him to the aisle where his listed item was and help him get it. After we got cart pushing mastered, he began the real shopping. By the end of the first year he could locate the items on his list if shown a duplicate and taken to the exact area of the aisle. By the end of the second year, he was able to be shown where his items were and then taken half the store's distance away and he could relocate them, pushing his basket carefully. Jimmy enjoyed this so much, but his mom didn't get the groceries home in very good shape. He was so rough with the bag and invariably she had potato chips on the list.

Jimmy's language picked up as his interest in other people increased, which makes sense. He used two to three words together by the end of the second year, but most of the time he still found that one word at a time would do it for him. He surprised us with an actual conversation a few times. Once, at the beginning of the second year, he walked up behind Mrs. McNulty, tapped her, and said, "Hi." She thought it was one of her fourth graders, and turned to answer. Jimmy pointed at the little aquarium filled with tadpoles which were rapidly turning into frogs, and said, "Fish."

Mrs. McNulty said, "Do you like fish, Jim?"

He answered, "Yes", and smiled. Now, **that** was a conversation!

I retired at the end of the second year Jimmy was in my class, and his mom wrote the following letter to me. I treasure it because, when I read it, I know I accomplished what I came to do when I decided to teach handicapped children, and I feel good!

Dear Barb,

I have started this letter six times. I want to express my appreciation for you and words aren't enough. There is so much emotion mixed in the gratitude that words seem incomplete. You have made such a difference in our lives. You make life easier for the parents and more enjoyable and fun for the kids.

When I think back to our first meeting, I remember thinking that you had such high expectations for Jimmy. They seemed totally impossible to me. I was terrified for him. So what if you had been teaching for 30 years! I was Mom and I just figured you didn't know Jimmy. Little did I know. What lessons Jimmy and I both learned.

Some of his goals seemed destined to failure. Grocery shopping, swimming, chores at school. I was nervous to say the least **but** failure is not in your vocabulary, is it? You see potential and possibilities-Can Do's, I call them! I am so thankful for that determination that exists within you.

We went to dinner tonight at Chevy's. We've never been there.

Jimmy just walked in like he was an old customer. Once we were seated, the waitress had put napkins and silverware in the middle of the table. Jim asked for his napkin to put it in his lap. Can you believe it? I remember when I couldn't take him anywhere where there would be a lot of people. He hated crowds and now it is nothing. We can go to any restaurant, store, or even the mall. It does not faze him.

Swimming was an impossible task as you and Cynthia found out rather quickly with sore necks from the Jimmy Death Grip! He would scream and howl the whole time he was near water, but now he swims like a fish. He dives for toys. He loves it!

You have taught me to expect more from him and being able to work along side you last year was something very special to me. It was an eye opener. You not only bring out the best in the kids with their capabilities, but you even do it with the parents. Thank you for that opportunity. It was a period of time I will treasure.

Summing It Up:

1. Let children become "teachers."
2. Assume success will occur. Don't limit or prejudge children.
3. Help parents raise expectations for their children.
4. Be patient; success **will** occur.

Chapter 2:

Mike

Mike was six years old and best described as "active but silent". He was in my Special Education classroom with 11 others, all designated *trainable mentally handicapped."* Mike was autistic, but a diagnosis of autism wasn't prevalent in our classes during the 1970's. He was content with his life and his schedule, but unfortunately his life and schedule didn't exactly fit with mine. He was silent when we had speech activities, but talked to himself non-stop during rest time; he was more than willing to sit in his chair if he needed to, but not when I wanted him to do some work at a table; he was happy to play with our free-time toys, but if he preferred the swings outside on the playground, he saw no problem with just running out to swing. He didn't share because he didn't acknowledge other children in the room. If another child had a toy Mike wanted, he simply took it, oblivious to the hand of the child currently holding it. He was interested in books, pictures, and certain objects, but he never tried to show me a picture or never looked up from a book laughing or pointing to a certain picture. He was "internalized" **big time**.

Mike was pudgy, with an angelic round face with very large intelligent brown eyes. He looked through people and focused intently upon things. When I spoke directly to him, his eyes scanned my face, but quickly moved on to more interesting sights, such as a toy or a book, or a spot on the wall. I tried working with Mike behind a screen to block his view of all those interesting objects, but it wasn't very effective. He did watch me a bit more, but he was still disconnected from me. I couldn't tell if he really heard me; there was never an appropriate reaction to my questions or to my instruction.

During free time in the classroom, Mike followed the other students into the play room area and usually chose the 4-piece farm animal puzzle that had a horse, a cow, a chicken, and a sheep. He only wanted the cow so he could manipulate it-not "play" with it, just "manipulate" it. The rest of the puzzle ended up on the floor. He chewed the cow, held it way above his head while he spun slowly around in circles, watching it every minute, rubbed it, waved it, and sometimes he ran with it. No matter what he chose to do with the cow, his eyes never left it.

One day Mike went into the play area and another child already had the farm animal puzzle. With the type of obsession he had for the cow, I knew this might be pretty interesting to watch. I thought Mike would grab it, but amazingly, he didn't. He stood next to the child who was on the floor, trying to fit the pieces in their proper places. He watched the cow piece. I was so fascinated because I could see that he wasn't watching anything else-not the child, not the futile attempts he was making to work the puzzle, nothing but the cow piece. It was as if he were interacting with it, mentally, and actually "playing" with it even though he wasn't able to have it. Mike never said a word, and hadn't talked ever during these first couple of weeks of school, except at rest time, but his arms were moving up and down, showing a little frustration.

Sometimes a crazy idea comes into my head and this puzzle piece fetish of Mike's gave me a winner of an idea. One day, after the students were gone, I removed the cow puzzle piece from the playroom and began using it to help teach Mike to focus on whatever I wanted him to look at. One of my academic goals for Mike was to demonstrate recognition by touching numerals given a choice of three. Up to this point, several weeks into the school year, I had made no headway getting him to actually look at the choices. I put a card with a 1 on the table, then about 6 inches away, I put a card with a 2 on it and about 6 more inches away I put a card with a 3 on it. Mike was oblivious to them until I suddenly produced the cow puzzle piece and his eyes were glued to it. He reached for it, but I pulled it back and told him to put his hands in his lap, which he did. The cow came back and I put it next to the #1 and said "**Look**" and he looked while I tapped the cow on the #1 and then I slid the cow along and stopped at the #2, "**Look!**" He looked while I tapped the cow on the #2, and then I slid the cow along again and stopped at the #3, "**Look!**" His eyes never left the cow.

Next I made the cow dance from one number to the next and then I said, "Mike, do you want the cow? " He reached for it, but I said, "Touch number 1" and you can have the cow. Touch #1". He did! I gave him the cow for a brief moment, and then took it back. "Mike, Touch #2. Here's the cow, Touch #2" and he did. I used this cow for all it was worth in every subject. What I discovered was that Mike already knew the numbers, the letters of the alphabet, and the basic colors and shapes. He went on to demonstrate recognition of many simple words, as well. Soon, Mike began reading many individual words.

To keep his attention, I used the cow in different ways. I hid a word strip under the cow and let him pick up the cow, but he had to read the word before I let him hold the cow for a few seconds. I also traced the cow shape several times on a piece of paper and wrote words he was learning to read on each cow and had him cover the word with his cow. At first, he didn't want to lay the piece down on the word, but I demonstrated how he could walk the cow from word to word reading as he went, and he liked that. I was so amazed at how much and how quickly he learned. He had definitely fooled us all and was obviously quite intelligent. We just needed a way to get his attention. That cow worked miracles.

Most children with autism have communication difficulties, and Mike was no exception. He could talk, because he always talked to himself during rest time, but rarely to other people. It was obvious that he was learning, but he wasn't going to be very successful in life without using speech appropriately. Mr. Bailey, the speech therapist was able to get Mike to go with him to the therapy room by using the cow to entice him, and he was able to finally get a few words out of him, but it was such a struggle. The therapist used a large doll to work on naming body parts and types of clothing. One day he brought Mike back before his therapy time was up. Mike had been sexually inappropriate with the doll! The therapist was shocked, and I was shocked. Mike was only 6 and he demonstrated knowledge he shouldn't have had.

It was a delicate topic, but I felt I needed to talk to Mike's mother about the incident. When I brought it up at my home visit, she was horrified but told me that he refused to sleep in his own bed and had been sleeping with her and her husband for about a year. That stopped, I'm sure. I always learned so much on my home visits and the information made my teaching more relevant for each child.

Mike's parents had heard him talk, but he rarely spoke directly to them. He sometimes communicated by taking their hand and showing them what he wanted, but usually he just took whatever he wanted wherever it might be. They had to watch him carefully because he seemed unaware of danger. When I asked what they hoped for him, they said they wanted him to talk to them in a meaningful way-ask questions, tell them what he wanted, etc. They also wanted to be able to trust him to stay with them when they were out in public. Mike was a runner. At school I didn't dare keep our classroom door open, because if he saw something outside he would run out of the door to get it. When we were on field trips, we always assigned an adult to be with him; we couldn't trust him to stay where he belonged.

Other than reading individual words and some short phrases, we didn't hear any spontaneous speech, until one day in March when we went to the park on a spring picnic. One of my helpers was a high school student who got credit for working one period a day in our room. In March, her class of 15 high school students decided to make a picnic lunch for my kids and we all walked to the nearby park for a fun time. We had 12 students in our class, the 15 "helpers" plus my aide, JoAnn and I, but about a dozen of the high school students were no help. They sat at the picnic tables and talked while JoAnn, my high school helper and I supervised the children in my class.

There was a lake at this park and after we finished eating, I planned for us to feed the ducks. I made the mistake of saying, "Let's clean up and **go feed the ducks**." I turned and heard the sound of running feet. I instantly knew it was Mike and when I turned back, he was running toward the lake filled with swimming ducks. No one else had noticed him. I took off running as fast as I could, but he was ahead of me and never even slowed down as he reached the shoreline. I was a second behind him, and in I went. I grabbed him and got out with him. The water wasn't very deep but we were both drenched. I was so upset and I hugged him, cried, and said, "Mike, you have to stay with Barb!"

He patted me on my back, and said, "It's okay, Barb, don't cry. Don't cry, it's okay, Barb, don't cry, don't cry." I was dumbfounded hearing so much language come out of his mouth and it was completely appropriate. There are these moments in teaching that you never forget.

After this, Mike talked more and more frequently. There were times over the next couple of months when I would be on the floor helping another child tie his shoe, or put together a puzzle and Mike would come up from behind and pat me and say, "It's okay, Barb" as if remembering the day my career flashed before my eyes.

Generally, children with autism fixate on something, such as the cow puzzle piece, for a length of time but then, overnight, it has no interest for them at all. It's strange, but I've seen that happen over and over again. However, in Mike's case, the cow held his strong attention during the entire school year. By the end of the year, the cow was minus a horn and was generally chewed and misshapen, but who cared? It was Mike's and my ticket to success.

Summing It Up:

1. Observe your students and use their interests to teach them. Be a creative observer.
2. Communicate with the parents. **Listen** carefully to them. Don't just deliver information, get information as well.
3. Remember that **you** are ultimately responsible for the safety of your students no matter how much help you may have. Be 100% attentive.
4. When speaking to very young children, remember that they will hear the last of what you say, so be careful how you end your sentences.

Chapter 3:

Bobby

Bobby bounced, and I mean that literally, in and out of my career for seven years. When I first saw him, he was holding his dad's hand as they walked into the classroom about a week after school had started. Some children come in for the first time and they are holding a parent's hand in fear, shyness, or some insecurity, but others, like Bobby, come in with the parent holding their hand. Once let go, Bobby was like an inflated balloon released flying around in every direction at once. My aide, Cynthia, struggled to handle the other eight children while his dad and I tried to capture Bobby. He was so **wild**! Before we could contain him, he had run headlong into the playroom and thrown himself so hard onto a couch that he actually flipped over the end of it and knocked over a shelving unit, scattering toys everywhere. When we caught him and his dad had his hand again, Bobby gave me a big smile and rocked his head rhythmically from side to side.

I taught Bobby four different school years from the time he was 7 until he was 14years old. At 7, he was a year older than most of my students in the primary class and he was the largest child in size and strength. Like many students with Downs Syndrome he had difficulty speaking clearly. He was almost unintelligible, but we soon understood him quite well. Pushing someone down meant he wanted what the other one had; watching someone and bobbing his head back and forth like a metronome meant he was content and enjoying what the other was doing; holding his head perfectly still while his eyes shone and his mouth smirked meant he was just about to do something mischievous. He seemed to love school and all of his classmates, but he was very rough with the materials, the furniture, and the children. He needed taming.

During academics, we divided the students into groups of two or three and the three adults in the room rotated from one group to the next. Bobby took pencils or crayons from the other students in his group, kicked others under the table, gave big bear hugs occasionally or burped in their faces. I began to notice that each time he hurt, tormented, or aggravated a classmate and the child cried, Bobby watched the injured child's face while smiling and rocking his head back and forth in happy fascination. He loved it. I constantly changed his position at the table, was sure he was next to me, with the wall of the classroom on his other side, and made him go back to the empty group table for a time out. I tried giving points, treats, little toys, and stickers. You name it, I tried it. Nothing really worked well.

One of the little girls in our class had cerebral palsy and, although she was able to walk, she had poor balance and her gait was very uneven, since one leg was so much shorter than the other. From minute one in that class, Bobby was fascinated by her. He loved watching her fall. If she didn't do it on her own, he helped her with a quick little push, followed by the contented side-to-side head bobbing. This became a huge issue. When we walked in line around campus, I made sure Erica was at the front or back of our line and he was at the other end, both with adults walking next to them. Everything went well most of the time, but we did have several other children with severe needs and occasionally the adults had to help them. This prompted Bobby to race for Erica and give her that little nudge. Over she'd go.

I tried everything I could think of to stop this behavior: punishment, extra supervision, and even bribery. I made him a card to carry and we put a nice sticker of an animal on it each time we walked in line and he stayed in his place, away from Erica. I thought it helped, but then, suddenly, we'd be distracted and off he'd go, straight for her, and push. Over she'd go again. One day, we had just left the classroom and he darted to her and pushed her into one of the pillars. I was beside myself. There are times like this, when you try so many different solutions and the one that ends up working is the absolute opposite of what you've been trying. When Erica fell into the pillar, she cried very hard and Bobby's head was still and he frowned, he looked upset, and then he actually sat on the sidewalk next to her. It occurred to me that he liked her, maybe loved her. He cared a lot about her. I could see it and feel it; suddenly, I found my answer. Instead of keeping him away from her, I told him to help her up, gave him a tissue and asked him to wipe her face to remove the dirt. He was super, super gentle. I put her hand in his and asked him if he would help her so that she couldn't fall down. I gave him the job of protecting her. It was one of the most amazing transformations of character I have ever witnessed in my career. All along, he wasn't really being mean. He liked her; she fascinated him. He was just curious and seemingly unaware that it could hurt her to fall down. It amused him greatly. Now, though, when she hit the pillar and cried, it upset him terribly. From that day on, Bobby was in charge of her safety. They were in the same class through their years in school and he always protected her. I taught him again when he was 9 and then 12 to 14 and he never stopped being her friend and helper.

A couple of school years later, when he was 9, Bobby and I reunited. The nickname I had for him was "Joker". His speech was still very poor, but he knew how to make himself understood a little better and he really loved a good joke. Many times a day he found something funny about others and usually it was due to some mistake. He found the shortcomings of any of us to be hysterical. He covered his mouth, giggled, and pointed at anyone who made any error, dropped anything, sneezed, coughed, tripped, or cried. A girl in our class named Sherry, also Downs Syndrome, became best friends with Bobby. They were just alike, a couple of pranksters.

Bobby had also become quite the thief, especially concerning food. He loved to eat and his fat tummy certainly proved that. He tried to get into the lunch boxes other students brought to school and during lunch he often grabbed food off other children's trays. He was lightning fast and grinned while he swallowed. He and Sherry often tried to take toys from the playroom by hiding items in their shoes. It was a little obvious as they hobbled along with little blocks in their shoes.

Each morning Cynthia and I met the special ed bus, but one morning in the spring of that year the driver opened the door and off walked Bobby and Sherry, stark naked! Even their feet were bare. We jumped on the bus and looked for their clothing, but nothing was there, except a wide open bus window. Just imagine the people driving behind that school bus as clothing, shoes and socks came flying out the window. Now, this was carrying their senses of humor just a bit too far! The nurse and her supply of extra clothing came to the rescue, and a very shaken bus driver left for the bus barn where he became a legend as the driver with the funniest bus story.

How to handle a joker? Well, laugh a lot, and deal with only the most serious situations. Stealing was my focus with Bobby during that year. I assigned jobs to all the children and his was to help my aide make sure all the toys were in their places on the free-time shelf. If he had taken anything, he usually put it where it belonged because he got a special sticker on his points card for doing this job.

I didn't have to even think of punishing him except for stealing food in the cafeteria. We put his seat next to the aide who went with the class to the cafeteria. This stopped about 90% of his thieving, but not all. My next step was to set up a small desk about five feet from our table in the cafeteria where Cynthia moved him and his food if he touched anyone else's food. Each day, as he was in line for lunch, the aide was instructed to say to Bobby "Eat only your food. " If he touched anyone else's food while inside, she repeated that and moved him to the desk. He had a lunch points card and got a special sticker each day that he was able to stay at the main cafeteria table. He had to give me the sticker card as soon as lunch was over and we discussed it very briefly. If he had to move to the desk, I'd point to the day spot on his card and say "Where is your sticker for today?" and make him explain as well as he could. If he had earned the sticker, I'd hug him and tell him he was a very nice boy to keep his hands to himself. If he got a sticker for all five days of the week, he earned a cookie. His mom was very cooperative and she provided the cookies. At first, he was sent to the desk frequently but rapidly improved ended the year eating a cookie most Fridays.

Two years later, when Bobby was in junior high, we were together again. Now, he weighed about 180 pounds, was about 5 feet 2 inches at best and was built like a sumo wrestler. I wasn't sure what had happened during the prior two years, but Bobby was now quite difficult to handle. He was big, strong, stubborn, silly, and starving most of the time. His head still bobbed back and forth when he was content, but it seemed to bob at some pretty inappropriate situations.

Bobby's aggression toward others was not actually mean-spirited; it was done more for his entertainment, just as it had been with Erica years earlier. Unfortunately, the recipient of a hard punch didn't find any joy in it, though, so it had to stop. We tried several plans, including a time out chair in the classroom, and there was improvement, but it had to totally stop.

I met with Bobby's mother and her suggestion was that we should involve food, since that was his greatest interest. We set up a program, approved by the principal that worked, and worked **fast**. I made a board with five hooks on it arranged horizontally and put it on the wall at the front of the class. On a hook next to the board I hung five index cards, each with a letter of the word L-U-N-C-H. There were five time slots before lunch during which Bobby could earn a letter simply by not being aggressive. He had a card with ten spaces on it, five on the top row and five on the bottom row. If he earned an L during the first time slot of the day, we hung it on the board and also wrote it on his card. If he earned the letter the second time slot, we hung a "U" on the board and wrote it on his card, and so on through the letters spelling entire word "LUNCH."

When we went to the cafeteria, he took the letter cards he had earned. Bobby had to give the "L" to get the main dish, the "U" to get the vegetable, the "N" to get the fruit, the "C" to get the bread and the "H" to get the dessert each day. He got the milk no matter what. There were days in the beginning when he only got the milk, but those days were rare. In the afternoon, he was able to earn the letters T-R-E-A-T which he took home with him to get his after-school treat from his mother. Through this home-school cooperation, we made a permanent change in Bobby. By the end of the first year, he earned the full lunch almost everyday. By the end of the second year, it was totally ingrained and he wasn't aggressive at all. I followed his progress and, although he always lived up to his nickname Joker, he wasn't hurting others.

To succeed, a behavior shaping program must be consistent. Sometimes, a glitch will show up and you will have to tweak the program quickly. We had to build in a consequence if Bobby didn't earn the bread or the dessert because they were his favorite parts of the meal, and he generally tried to take the bread or dessert from a nearby tray. If that happened, he lost his entire lunch and was done. This worked very well, but one day Cynthia had to remove his tray and when she turned her back, he jumped onto her back, hitting her. Several of the staff rushed to her defense and they removed him from the cafeteria. He was on the grass outside and wouldn't get up. They called me from my lunch. I walked out there and told him to get up, which he did. He and Cynthia walked to the classroom with me, and Bobby walked right over to the time-out chair, crying with total remorse. Cynthia sat at one of the tables and cried. It was a pitiful situation, but became a remarkable turning point. Bobby had always loved her and he was very upset with himself. The principal sent him home for three days as a punishment. For three days, he had no snacks at home and his dad gave him a shovel and told him to start digging. After a day and a half of digging for many hours a day, his dad told him to start filling in the hole. With this type of cooperation from Bobby's parents, Bobby learned a great lesson. From that traumatic day forward, Bobby followed the plan and his aggressiveness steadily decreased and eventually disappeared.

Summing It Up:

1. Laugh a lot. It will get you through a lot of crazy situations.
2. Control seating to help alleviate potential problems.
3. Observe misbehaving students very carefully to help you decide motives. The motive will determine the behavior plan.
4. Work with parents and principals when setting up severe or controversial behavior plans.
5. Communicate clearly with parents about the student's progress on behavior plans.
6. Be proactive and not reactive. State the rule briefly and prior to the time you see the possibility of misbehavior.

7. Maintain the behavior plan long after it seems to have succeeded. Let the good behavior become a habit.

8. Be consistent but be humane. No matter how bad a behavior, there are no "bad" children.

Chapter 4:

Ben

After I retired the first time and moved to a small town, I took a job in the special education preschool at the local elementary school where I met Ben. We had too many children in the program and too little space, but that didn't bother Ben. During free choice time he always found a flat surface somewhere and worked his puzzles very, very quickly-one after the other. He was 4, not toilet- trained, had no expressive language that I ever heard during those weeks, had no relationship at all with any children, but he was very sweet, well behaved, and caused absolutely no trouble. At recess, he wanted to be pushed on the swings. It was the only interaction I ever saw him initiate in that program. He ran outside, ran up to an adult, and pulled her toward the swings. He was autistic and very disinterested in the rest of us!

Ben's strong interest in being pushed on the swings gave me a wonderful tool to help him try to talk. I was hired with only eight weeks of school remaining and each day at recess Ben took my hand and led me to the swings. Once he was sitting on the swing, ready for fun, I'd pull him back and say, "Do you want me to push? Are you ready? Say 'puh' (the 'p' sound)." In the beginning his legs flailed when I didn't release him, but no "p" sound was uttered. I'd lower him, get in front of him at eye level and say, "Ben, do you want to swing?" and he'd start pumping his legs in response. "You have to tell me what to do, Ben! Ben! Say 'puh.'" I'd repeat this three or four times, pulling him up high, ready for the big release, but when I got no "puh", I finally just went to another child and made him say "Push" and I'd keep him going. Ben showed a lot of quiet irritation.

After a couple of weeks, I was so thrilled to hear that 'p' sound and I pushed him several times, then would stop the swing high in the back stroke and make him say 'puh' again. After this got commonplace, I expanded to trying to get 'puh shhhh'—two definite sounds. He picked it up after only one day of not getting pushed. By the end of those eight weeks, he said "push" very clearly each time he wanted to be pushed. What I didn't realize at the time was that Ben had high end autism and actually was quite capable of talking, but he had no desire or need to do it. He hadn't connected his ability with the need. Ben lived with his grandparents who were very conscientious. They were thrilled with the "push" success and decided to hire me as a tutor for him during the summer.

I tutored Ben once a week for the next eight years. By the end of the first summer he was not only talking, but reading too. He surprised us all.

My sessions that summer were the same each week. When I arrived, we immediately took a walk beginning with his front yard where we walked to a very tall cypress tree, touched it, and said "tree." Then we bent down to the flowers and smelled one and said "flower," then walked to the street and sat on a big rock at the beginning of the neighbor's yard, and said "Sit," and then we patted the rock and said "rock".

We then walked around the corner and down a farmer's access road. There were cows and horses and a goat in the field and for each animal we stopped, pointed and said "horse" or "cow" or "goat". At the end of the access road was an open area in the trees where we could see Ben's house and we pointed and said "house". As we walked back, we looked for new things, such as an ant bed, some other bug, a cat, a special flower, a puddle after a rain, or some other item of interest. When we got back to his house, we stopped at the mailbox, said "open" and opened the mailbox. To end the walk, he ran to his tree swing in his yard and I pushed him if he said "push." After the walk, we went into his house and made a book of pictures about what we had seen and I wrote a little phrase about each thing, for example, "a tall tree" or "a big horse." I read each phrase and held his finger to touch each word. At the end of each session, his grandmother came in and we "read" the book to her.

At the beginning of June, I was lucky to get an initial sound of a few of the words, but by the end of June, he was saying each of the words and knew the walking route perfectly. When we wrote our book he was starting to repeat each word of the phrase I wrote. By the end of July we had expanded the language for each of our stops. Now, it was "tall tree," "yellow flower," "sit down," "big rock," etc. By the end of August, he was able to label each stop without hearing it first and in many cases he used two or three word phrases, such as "a tall tree." By that point, he was touching the words in the phrases as he "read" them to his grandmother.

I decided to try an experiment and I wrote the single words we were using on separate cards, shuffled them, and flashed them. He read every word. He was 4 and hadn't been talking three months earlier. It was so exciting. Once school started, he went back to the same preschool but I had a job at a different school. His grandmother was very excited about this progress and wanted me to continue. I decided to teach him to read using a sight reading program I had used during my main career. By Christmas, he had a base of 150 words and could read stories a page or two long using words from that list. It became so obvious that he had a lot of information inside of him, but he hadn't communicated it, but that was changing rapidly.

By the time Ben was a second grader, he was a total magpie chatterbox. He never stopped talking and was obsessed with certain subjects. For a long time it was cars, then dogs, then geography. He was in general education classes but scored low in reading comprehension. It was frustrating because he could read quickly and could retell a story, but he couldn't answer the most simple, obvious questions about the story. I worked a long time on reading comprehension in general, but finally started making progress by writing sentences that contained *who, what, where,* and *when* answers. I saved *why* for later.

An example of one of these sentences is "A boy saw a cloud in the sky today." By rote, I taught him to look for a person or animal to answer a *who* question; a thing to answer a *what* question, a time, a day, a month, a year, or a word like today, tomorrow, or yesterday for a *when* question and a place for a *where* question. We worked only on *who* questions through many sentences until he was getting the correct answer every time. Next, we worked on *what* until he always got it right. After that, we worked on mixing up the *who* and *what* questions. When that was 100%, we worked on *where* and then mixed *who, what,* and *where.* Then we moved onto *when* and finally mixed all four. Once he understood this concept, I used his library books to ask the questions.

Ben's brain was really interesting. He was a natural speller. When he was 7 or 8 and learning to write paragraphs I was amazed at the words he could spell. He seemed to intuitively know when to spell an "f" sound with a "ph", or knew to spell a word like "famous" using the "ous" instead of just a "us." I couldn't figure it out until I realized he had a photographic memory. Once he had seen a word, he knew how to spell it. He always made it quite far in the school spelling bees.

His real talent, however, was in geography. He **loved** maps. He was given atlases as gifts because his old ones would be threadbare from having the pages turned so many times. There are over 200 counties in Texas and he could name them all, even though he lived in Arizona. He knew obscure facts about every state. Here was a conversation we had one evening before I was to leave on a vacation to the east coast.

Ben: "Are you going through Texas?"

Barb: "Yes, but just the top part"

Ben: "Are you going to be in Dallam County?"

Barb: "I don't know, Ben, I really don't know the counties in Texas."

Ben looked at me incredulously. I got my atlas out when I got home and there it was! Dallam County, is the most northwestern county in Texas. Amazing! Ben was 9 and not only knew the Texas counties by name and location but he knew all of the counties of many states. Because of his photographic memory and his obsession with atlases, he knew all 50 states, their state birds, flowers, trees, nicknames, location in the country, famous residents, slogans, mottoes, historical facts, dates of entry, and so on before he was 8. He couldn't get enough of geography. When he was in the seventh grade, he was the geography bee champion from his county and went to the state competition where he did very well. Two weeks before the state bee, I asked him how he was studying for it. "I'm not studying. I know it." He didn't stress one second about it. He just knew it and loved knowing it, and if he didn't win, he didn't care. During the questioning, he was asked to name African countries surrounding the Sudan. He had no difficulty. I couldn't have begun to do it.

One of my difficulties while tutoring Ben was that he only wanted to talk to me, not work on writing or reading comprehension, which were his weaker areas in school. One day I walked in and he immediately said, "Your hair is browner!" and off we went talking about my hair turning gray, how often I had to dye it, why I dyed it, and on and on.

In between each question, I would try to get his focus back on track, but it was almost impossible. He asked questions faster than I could answer them and if I had let him, he would have questioned me all hour long every week. Ben was a genius if interested in a topic and he never forgot what he learned, but he couldn't seem to retain information if he didn't find it interesting. He ignored it and forgot it and didn't care. That ended up being my ticket to teaching him information he needed but didn't care about learning. I had to pair what I wanted to teach with what he wanted to know.

I wanted to teach him to write paragraphs so when we sat down to work and he said, during his obsession with cars, "Do you still LOVE your Nissan?"

I said, "Do you want to know if I love my Nissan, Ben? I'll tell you as soon as you write this title on this paper," and I handed him the paper and said our topic was 'My Best Friend'."

He asked again, "But, do you LOVE your Nissan?"

I pointed at the top line of the paper and said, "I'm ready to answer but first you have to write the title, 'My Best Friend'." He wrote it. "Yes, I really **love** my Nissan. It's a good car. Who is your best friend?"

His answer was another question, "Why do you always buy Nissans?"

I said, "Why? Oh, I like that question! First, who is your best friend, Ben? Hurry and tell me so I can tell you about why I love Nissans, hurry."

Now, he was excited and said, "Johnny R. We have a Johnny N and a Johnny R, but I like Johnny R the best."

As he answered, I wrote what he said and then answered, "I have a friend named John, too. I like to buy Nissans because we never have any car trouble. Here's your first sentence to write. Remember to indent."

He said, "Did you ever have a Ford?"

I said, "A Ford? That's a story I'll tell you. First, hurry and write your first sentence. It's your topic sentence." As he copied his sentence, I said, "What do we call this first sentence, Ben?" He concentrated on writing the sentence and I said, "Topic sentence." When he finished writing, I said, "What do we call that sentence, Ben? Tell me so I can tell you my story about the Ford." He said, "Topic sentence," almost under his breath, and looked at me with anticipation.

"My Ford was a hunk of junk!"

He laughed and said, "Did it break?"

I responded, "It sure did. Do you want to know what broke?" Of course he did, but I added "First, though, what do you like to do with Johnny R?"

"Play", he said.

"Play what?" I countered.

"Play on the slide and monkey bars."

I wrote a second sentence for him to copy. "Write this detail sentence and I will be ready to tell you what broke on my Ford." He wrote it very quickly.

This became my method and it ended up working well. I started making him work a little longer between questions and answers. In the beginning, I was thrilled to get a topic sentence, one detail sentence and a conclusion. Writing was never his love, but he certainly improved a great deal. By sixth grade, we got to the point that I wrote down his questions and at the end of the writing project, we had a great conversation and I answered all his non-stop questions. I always wanted to find a topic he loved enough to enjoy writing about, but that didn't happen until he was in high school. He started writing letters to the editor of the local paper about **politics**. Priceless.

Summing It Up:

1. If a child has obsessive compulsive behaviors, use his obsession to reach and teach him.

2. Continue raising your expectations, starting at a level of easy success while having your eye on the level you are planning to reach.

3. When you require a certain behavior, base it on a certainty that the student is able to achieve it, and then be completely consistent.

4. When dealing with children with autism, realize that you have to work hard to break into their world. Make it worth their while. Be funny, animated, loving, silly, or whatever it takes! It will be so worth it.

5. Show respect and admiration for the student's achievement and knowledge. Be amazed by amazing effort.

Chapter 5:

Mandy

About two weeks after school started, I took my group of moderately mentally handicapped students on a field trip. We had been having quite a bit of rain, so I thought it would be fun if the children brought their own umbrellas in case we had rain that morning. I got a call from Mandy's mom, who told me that she had tried to send the umbrella, but Mandy was terrified of umbrellas and had taken it out of her backpack and left it on the lawn when the bus came to pick her up. I listened to this and gave it only a tiny bit of concern, since I had brought several umbrellas in case any child forgot his. That morning, before time for us to leave, I started having a lesson on how to open and close and use the umbrella safely and that's when the chaos started. Mandy cried and refused to hold an umbrella. She started backing up toward the classroom door. When I retrieved her and tried to have her walk with me under the umbrella she cried and screamed, covering her ears with both hands. The teacher next door opened our adjoining door to see who was being killed! Mandy was okay if she didn't have to touch it or walk under it, so we went on the trip minus one umbrella.

Each month a student of the month was chosen from each classroom in our elementary school. Students were selected for demonstrating that month's valued character trait, such as honesty. Mandy was our student of the month for September. She was perfectly behaved, a joy to teach, excited by every activity, a good listener, and liked by everyone. When I had my home visit with her mother, I asked her one of my standard questions. Is there anything you would like us to work on to make life easier for you at home? At that, the floodgates opened and Mandy's mother started telling me how terrified Mandy was of anything over her head like an umbrella, a hood of a jacket, a canopy, or especially a tent. She said their family loved to camp and it was so hard on everyone that they rarely went, and they had started leaving Mandy with her grandparents. It was frustrating, also, on a rainy day because Mandy wouldn't get under an umbrella and wouldn't allow a hood to be on her head. Her mom had no idea why Mandy was so frightened, but said it had started when Mandy was very young—about 3 or 4. As I drove home that evening, I thought hard about this problem, trying to imagine what I might do to help.

Desensitizing a child who has an irrational fear was something I had done several times through the years, so I decided to try it with Mandy by having the students decorate a large teepee that we would keep in the center of the classroom. Everyone loved it, everyone, that is, except Mandy. She was willing to decorate the flat material, but once it took on the shape of a tent, she was finished with it. We did several things inside the tent daily. Each child placed his backpack inside the tent each morning, and at the end of each day we all sat in a circle inside the tent and went over the daily points cards, and the children got rewards.

Mandy began by crying, holding her hands over her ears, and sitting way across the room. I was hoping the laughter, fun, and pleasure the other children exhibited would encourage her, entice her, intrigue her-but, no. When it was time to line up to go home, she needed to get her backpack and she certainly wasn't going to leave it with us, so I held her hand and walked her to the tent's opening where I had her backpack straddling the entryway. She grabbed it and hurried to get in line.

I needed to reassess what to do because I wasn't getting anywhere. The other children loved the tent, but Mandy hated it. I decided to have our snack inside the tent each afternoon and I gave Mandy the permanent job of passing out the graham crackers. She was such a well behaved child and loved having a special job so I hoped for the best. I also put a chair about 10 feet in front of the tent's opening and told her to sit in it as soon as she passed out the crackers. The other students stood in front of the tent and as soon as Mandy handed out the crackers, they went inside and sat down. She sat in her chair but could see inside the tent. I moved her chair a little closer every few days. She quickly was willing to walk up to the tent, pass out the crackers, and then would go back and sit in her chair. The chair kept getting closer but she didn't start to complain until the chair was about 3 feet in front of the door.

I told a story while the students ate their crackers inside the tent and Mandy seemed to listen and watch very closely. The next time I moved the chair, it was right outside of the door. She was very nervous, but so well behaved that when I told her to sit down, she did, but her hands were over her ears. The good news was that she didn't cry.

Every Thursday our class went into the community for a leisure activity, lunch at a restaurant, and grocery shopping. Our leisure activity in January and February was camping and hiking and we pitched a tent several times. Mandy was a nervous wreck, but with my aide staying right with her and encouraging her she was willing to help set up the tent. That was a big step, and I really thought we might get her inside, but when the tent rose up, she ran over to the picnic table, turned her back to the tent, and whimpered.

I sat down with her and calmly talked to her about the tent and what the students were doing. "Look at Bill, Mandy. He's opening the windows on the tent. Joey just took the blanket into the tent. What's he going to do with it, Mandy?" She started answering my questions and observing everything that went on at the tent. Finally, I was able to get her to walk over to it with me and look in the window at the kids inside. Our PE teacher sat inside the tent with the other students and told a story. Mandy listened through the window, laughing at the funny parts, and was very relaxed.

In January I started putting Mandy's backpack and coat inside the tent far enough that she had to actually lean into the tent to get them. She did it! That was a wonderful day for me. I started to believe we just might get her inside before the year was over. About the middle of January I put a sucker for her just beyond her reach inside the teepee. She leaned way in, but couldn't quite get it. It was almost the end of January when we had our best day. Mandy stepped in with one foot and it allowed her to reach the sucker. I was so excited and so was she.

I found out at the beginning of February that her family was moving to another city. She was such a delightful little girl and I just know she would have gone completely in that tent if I had had her for the full year. It might have taken two years, but we could have succeeded—I know it!

Summing It Up:

1. Be happy with baby-step progress. It all adds up to a giant leap.

2. Be positive even when it seems hopeless. Believe it will happen and guess what? It will!

3. Don't get discouraged if the time you have with a student ends before you feel "finished." Be proud of your part in the continuum.

Chapter 6:

Bev

Sometimes you get a student who is just so great and so well-behaved and who learns easily that you have to be careful to not lose her in the shuffle. The first day of school in 1975 brought that student to my classroom. She was 5, had Downs Syndrome, was chunky, and had big blue eyes, a broad, sweet smile, long blond curls and an incredible speech problem caused by her oversized tongue, typical of many people with this syndrome. I asked her name and she tried very hard to say "Beverly" but it was completely unintelligible.

She started checking out the toys in the room and as I watched her, she went up to several of the other children, put her cute face right in front of theirs and rattled something to them. Since the children couldn't understand a word she said, they just continued playing and ignored her. I felt so sorry for her, at first, but that didn't last because I began to realize that she wasn't about to give up on these new friendships. She went to another child, tried talking, got nowhere, and then took his hand and went over to the couch in the playroom, patted the seat, and both of them jumped up there. I've known Bev for 35 years and she still won't be denied, won't be overlooked, and won't ever give up at something she wants to do.

When I had my first home visit with Bev's parents, we discussed her tremendous speech problems. I asked if they always called her Beverly and they said that they had. I suggested we shorten it to Bev to make it easier for her to say and to learn to write it. They supported this major change without any hesitation and from that day forward she was always Bev. Good communication with parents, on a comfortable level like at their home, can be so effective. I admired Bev's parents so much for making this change for her benefit. I worked with her for many years, suggested many things, and her parents usually saw the advantage for Bev and readily agreed.

When Bev was 10 and I was at our home visit, I talked about the importance of being able to start leaving her alone for brief amounts of time and being able to trust her while she was alone. This was always a scary goal for parents, but we worked out a plan for Bev, and her parents implemented it. Her mom would turn the TV on and tell Bev that she had to go somewhere in the car and Bev needed to sit and watch TV until she came home. She couldn't go outside, answer the door, or the phone while she was alone. Mom left, started the car, backed out and pulled up in front of the house before she came back in. Although she had never left, Bev thought she had. She was praised for being good while Mom was gone. We planned weekly increases in the amount of time Bev's mom was gone and she followed the schedule, becoming more comfortable as the weeks progressed. After several weeks, she left the house, drove around the block and sat in the car for several minutes before re-entering the house. Building trustworthiness is difficult whether it is training a young or handicapped child to be alone or whether it is teaching students to turn in assignments, go on errands at the school, or study for tests. You can't just expect it to come naturally to all children. Building the "responsibility" skill step by step will assure success.

Bev was learning to read but it was a very slow process. Our school had a reading teacher who pulled the students one at a time from the classroom to teach an individualized program. Bev had shown slow, but steady progress until age 11 when she just seemed to plateau, maintaining the skills without progressing. The reading teacher scheduled a meeting to let me know of her decision to discontinue the reading program with Bev. I didn't agree so continued her reading instruction in the classroom. Considering that her mental age was only 6 to 7 at the time, I couldn't see giving up yet.

I was right. Bev maintained a slow but steady climb toward becoming a reader. By the time she was 14 and ready for our junior high program she was reading between first and second grade level. The junior high teacher again wanted to discontinue reading instruction and concentrate on practical life skills. There certainly wasn't anything wrong with the life skills curriculum but Bev loved to read and her parents wanted her to continue instruction. They asked me to attend the planning meeting and we placed reading instruction in her plan.

Individualizing instruction is very important and it turned out to be critical for Bev. Being an advocate for your student, even after she's left your class, is also critical. When Bev was in the last years of high school, her job coach got her a job at a Montessori School where she read to the preschoolers, swept, cleaned bathrooms, and helped supervise on the playground. One of my greatest thrills was to listen to Bev read each card she received at her high school graduation party. She is past 40 now and is able to correspond via email and can read the emails sent to her. She also likes to read "chapter" books. Children can always learn more than they currently know and teachers should never give up on them. Some children plateau, but it shouldn't be thought of as the end of the path; it's just a wide spot. They reach goals at different rates, but given the chance, most will reach them successfully.

There was a convenience store about two blocks away from Bev's home, but it was across a very busy road. When she was about 13, I suggested to her parents that she needed to learn to go the store. This included getting there and returning safely, purchasing by paying correctly and bringing home the correct change. We set up a plan involving a gradual diminishing of parental protection. At first, her mom and Bev walked together to the corner of the busy street, crossed safely with the light, bought an item at the store and returned home safely. After a few days of that, her mom started walking behind Bev all the way, helped her understand how to get the item at the store, pay correctly, and receive the correct change, and then she followed her home. After a short while, her mom started out first and waited at the end of each block and finally across the busy street. Increasing Bev's responsibility occurred slowly as her mom felt comfortable. Eventually, Bev went this route to the store and also to her job at the Montessori School. There's no greater gift to give any child than independence and responsibility and no greater responsibility than to be sure it is learned safely!

After she graduated from high school, Bev worked full time at the Montessori School and is still employed there today, 17 years later. She receives her paycheck, deposits it at the bank, and uses a debit card. She writes checks as needed, buys her own clothes, pays for her travel expenses, and even treats her old teacher to lunch every now and then.

Summing It Up:

1.   Help parents help their children. Part of your role will be to guide parents. Sometimes this will be with school issues, sometimes with social issues.

2. Help children become as independent and responsible as possible.

3. Involve parents in ways that will advance the child's skills in school or out.

4. Be careful not to overlook the well behaved children. The students with problems can take up a lot of time, so be cautious.

5. You don't have to agree with other teachers, experts, authors, or school authorities. Use your common sense and always think about what is best for students when deciding on curricular changes.

Chapter 7:

Donald

It was the first day of school and while I talked to my class of primary mentally handicapped kindergarteners, I watched a diminutive little 5 year old boy watching me. His dark brown eyes were so big and so bright and seemed to be saying, "Quit talking and let's have fun!" When I kept talking, he decided to have the fun on his own and just got up and left! He ran right out of the classroom. My aide, Jane, was right behind him and brought him back to his place at the table and she sat right behind him.

"You need to stay right here in your chair, Donald", I said, and then it started.

He spoke in a run on sentence that went on and on and on. His voice was very high and squeaky and oozed excitement. It went something like this: "I went outside I want to play and I went outside and what are we going to do are we going to play in the playhouse where's my mom (turning to the child next to him and grabbing his nametag) this is your name where's my name here's my name." That was the start of my three years with Donald. He was my talker!

Donald loved tractors. That's all I needed to know to keep his attention, which usually lasted about a tenth of a second. With a toy tractor, a picture of a tractor, sound effects of a tractor, or even saying the word *tractor*, I had his undivided attention. I put the word out for farm magazines so I could have a big supply of tractor pictures and I went to a tractor company and got catalogs just for the pictures. Donald's hyperactivity was expressed with every part of his body; his head always bobbed, his arms and legs moved constantly, his eyes flicked from one view to the next at breakneck speed. Although testing him was a trick, I discovered he was quite proficient at identifying in all the basic pre-academic areas such as alphabet letters, numerals, colors, and shapes, but he couldn't label any of them. This inability was so pervasive and persistent, no matter how many creative approaches I tried, that I began to realize that his problem was a real learning disability. This, on top of the fact that his IQ was in the mentally handicapped range, made teaching him the names of letters, numerals, colors, and shapes so much harder. Most mentally handicapped children learn slowly, but they learn sequentially and logically. Donald had a complicated learning problem. His retardation caused learning to occur slowly but his learning disability made it a much greater challenge. Because I wasn't experienced enough at the time, I didn't hit upon a solution for two years. Fortunately, I taught Donald for four years.

During years one and two I tried many things. It took awhile to realize what the problem seemed to be and then for the rest of that first year I drilled at the labeling level. One approach, usually very successful, was the 5 card technique. I flashed a card, let's say, the color red, 5 different times during which I said, "red, what color is it?"

Donald said, "red."

Each time I flashed the card, I moved its position to encourage Donald to really look at it. After the fifth time, I'd say, "What's your name?"

"Donald," he'd quickly reply.

Then, I flashed the red card a sixth time and said, "What color is this?"

He might say "black," "white." "green," whatever came to his mind-maybe even "red" but I could tell it was just a guess.

When I interrupted his sequential responses, he forgot the correct answer. I continued this, as well as bombarding him with activities involving the colors, shapes, numbers, or letters, but with no serious success.

Donald got a little black Chihuahua dog, a very yappy little dog I had the misfortune to meet during my home visit at the beginning of my third year with him. His name was "Chico" and he made talking to Donald's parents very difficult. The day after my conference, I was telling the other children about going to Donald's house and meeting "Yappy Chico" as I called him. To encourage longer sentences from Donald, I asked him to tell the other kids about his new puppy. As he talked, one of the students asked Donald what color his puppy was and Donald immediately said he was black. As I listened to Donald talk about that yappy black puppy, I got the idea that ended up being the answer to his problem. It can be so frustrating while you search for the way to teach a child but so exhilarating when you finally figure it out.

When it was time to work on naming colors with Donald, I flashed the black card and said, "What color is this, Chico?_____"

Donald said, "Black."

That was our beginning. I paired every color with something familiar to him and pretty soon our tests went quickly: "fire fire red," "sunny sunny yellow," "Barb's hair brown," "Chico black", "snowman white", and so on. After he was able to get 100% three or four times in a row on all 10 colors, I started dropping the cue word. If he couldn't think of the color, I just said the beginning sound of the cue word or some other little clue, such as "ch" sound and he would say "black." It sounds so silly, but within a couple of months he was naming all the colors with absolutely no hints. At first I had difficulty trying to figure what to say for the numerals but then I drew a person with 1 head, 2 arms, 2 legs, 3 buttons, 4 earrings, 5 fingers, 6 rings, 7 bows in her hair, 8 toys, 9 hats and 10 toes. He loved the drawing which I drew during every lesson. I flashed the number card, for instance #1, and eventually he'd say, "One head", just from memory, and I'd draw that part. When I flashed #2, he'd say "2 arms, 2 legs", etc. Once he learned the numerals in order, I started mixing them up and he was amazing. He thought it was funny when I started with #10 and drew the toes first.

For the alphabet letters I drew a funny cartoon picture of something that started with the letter and paired that with the word and the letter. Then I gradually dropped the picture and used just the word and then finally was able to drop the word, just as I had with the color. Letter "T" was our easiest letter to learn because "T" was "tractor T." Once I realized that Donald was an auditory learner who needed sounds, words, etc. paired with visual symbols to retain what he learned, we made fast progress.

By the end of the fourth year that Donald and I were together, he was beginning to read many sight words. Initially, they needed to have an importance to Donald but by that time he was 8 and maturing a bit. He realized that the totality of the words had a meaning and that helped him remember. Of course, his first sight word was *tractor* and then we found other words to go with his favorite word. He could read "A big yellow tractor" within one week and then we were really cooking.

Summing It Up:

1. When working with young children or children with attention deficits, try to find out what they are **very** interested in as

quickly as you can. Ask parents and observe the child. Once you know the interest, you will have a better chance of holding the child's attention.

2. If you feel the child has some barrier to learning, think creatively to find a technique that works with this particular child. You may need to brainstorm with other teachers to help you but the most important thing for you to do is to pay attention to the child and he will undoubtedly lead you to the answer.

3. Once you find a technique, develop an organized sequential approach from the beginning steps of your interesting new technique to the skill you are trying to teach.

4. All children have learning styles. Find the best for each child, especially for those having difficulty learning traditionally.

5. Never give up searching for the most effective way to teach. Don't be a lazy teacher. Be a dynamic Teacher!

Chapter 8:

Frank

Frank's mom came to Back-to-School Night with Frank in a child's umbrella stroller, even though he was 9 and a big, husky boy. The stroller looked well worn and I was quite amazed that he could fit in it. Frank had cerebral palsy, couldn't walk, had poor hand control, could only say a few words and spoke those very slowly, but he showed the same excitement most children show when they come to meet their new teacher. His smile was so radiant and his joy so obvious that he caught my attention. As I reached for his hand to say hello and let him know how happy I was to meet him, he got so excited that he squealed, arched his back and flailed his other arm which smacked me on my shoulder and nearly catapulted himself out of that flimsy stroller.

During the first year Frank was in my class he graduated to a wheelchair but he was unable to maneuver it at all because of his weak right arm. He grew to be a very large 10-year-old, and it was difficult to lift him in and out of the chair. I used to be amazed at the strength his mother demonstrated, but she had been building those muscles as he grew. Even she realized, though, that he was destined to be a large man like his dad.

She talked to me about the idea of getting an electric wheelchair that he could drive himself. His therapists hoped that his skills would develop to the point he could safely use an electric chair, but they stressed that he was a few years from that point. They set up exercises for us to do in the classroom. He had a joy stick, similar to the one on an electric wheelchair, and it made a toy car go forward, backwards, or to the right or left. Frank had a ball with it, making that little red car bounce around our class doing some pretty wild tricks, but he didn't seem to comprehend how to control its direction.

Frank's mom and I both started noticing Frank's frustration at his lack of mobility. If his tray was off his chair, and he was pushed up to a table, he would use his left hand to push himself backwards and pull himself forward again, and his laughter rang out. It was his favorite game. He demonstrated poor hand control, even with the left hand, in many ways. He invariably spilled his drinks in his attempt to reach for his cup. I knew how important it was to Frank's family for him to get more independence so we increased the amount of time we worked with the joy stick, but the connection between his manipulation of it and the direction of the toy car just didn't seem to click. He sure had fun with it, though. To him, it was strictly a great toy.

By the end of our second year together, Frank's mother was convinced that he would be able to operate an electric wheelchair if given the chance, so she bypassed the therapists and filled out all of the paperwork to be eligible for help getting him the chair at a reduced price. He got the chair at the beginning of my third year with him.

Frank didn't surprise the therapists, he flabbergasted them! Within the first hour with his chair, he understood the direct correlation between the joy stick and his freedom. Within the first hour he and I walked and rode through all of the hallways of our school, with Frank greeting everyone who passed by. It might not have been wise to get directly in front of him on that first day, but he did remarkably well at stopping, starting, and turning right or left. He had trouble judging when to start turns, but within the first week he could control the chair well enough to stay in our line, although we usually had him at the front of it to prevent any accidents with other children. Before a couple of weeks passed, we actually sent him from our classroom to the office alone, although one of my aides went to the office first and watched for him.

The therapists were astounded and wondered why he had always done so poorly with the car, but they weren't thinking logically, in my opinion, because he was very successful with the joystick by making the car do all kinds of fun things. He didn't connect it with the joystick for the wheelchair because he had no idea about the existence of an electric wheelchair or what it could mean for his independence and happiness. Once he was placed in one and shown how to make it go by himself, he realized instantly what it meant. For the first time in his 11 years, he could move himself, unaided, and he was "off and rolling."

During the last two years I taught Frank, he refined his finesse with his chair, so he could position himself so that his left side was parallel to anything he needed to reach. When we went to the grocery store each week during our community functioning activities, he drove around the store in search of an employee, showed his grocery list and asked, "Help me, please," and then drove along with the employee to the correct aisle. In the community, we taught him to look for the Handicap Accessible symbol and for ramps, to help him remain independent. Although mentally handicapped, and severely physically handicapped, he learned all of these lessons quickly because he needed to. He seemed to realize the importance of each lesson.

There were several times when his battery died and he had to wait for a replacement or times his chair needed a repair and Frank became despondent. He never quite understood why his wheels had been taken away, thus forcing him to be in the old chair that he couldn't move a single inch. It was sad to see him just sitting with his head hanging. Once, after about three weeks without his independence, Frank got his chair back and we were at the skating rink during our community functioning activities. He drove out onto the rink and while skaters whizzed around him, he put on a show. He rode in circles. He went forward, backwards, and did figure eights. He was able to personally decide what he wanted to do and he was able to make it happen, alone. I will never forget the huge smile on that boy's face.

Summing It Up:

1. Make lessons relevant to the student.
2. Listen to parents. They know their children best.
3. A child's experience determines how he learns. You may take for granted that he understands what you are teaching, but his lack of experience or maturation might alter the outcome.
4. Our goal in education is always to help children become independent adults.

Chapter 9:

James

I couldn't believe a 5-year-old could terrorize a classroom and cause ordinarily sane adult teachers to say they detested a little child, but James did it. I was working as a consultant after 35 years of teaching, and part of my role in that district was to hire and train aides for the special ed teachers. One day, I was called down to the class for emotionally disabled students and James was literally straddling an 8 foot tall rolling room divider and no one could get him down. He was screaming obscenities of the "drunken sailor" type. As I opened the classroom door, the teacher and two aides were pulling on his legs while one other aide tried to control the four other children in the room. She couldn't. It was chaos.

James had four siblings who were also in special ed and his parents were also slow, making it difficult for them to help James. He had absolutely no home support. He didn't have a bed; he slept on a pallet on the living room floor. There were fleas on the dogs that hopped onto James and then hopped off of James onto his desk at school. He rarely bathed and wore the same clothes for a week at a time.

He spent most of his time at home playing a very violent video game that celebrated "cop killing", bombs, gunfire, and all sorts of mayhem. At school, he vacillated between asking amazing, interesting questions and screaming obscenities while hitting or spitting on other children. He had to have an aide with him constantly to protect the other children and he had a 1:1 aide on the bus. His behavior worsened as he grew older. He became frighteningly aggressive. Counselors, teachers, special behavioral coaches, and police all worked with James, to very little avail.

One thing about him didn't change, though, and that was his never-ending list of questions. He wanted to talk about guns, bombs, death, and destruction. He wondered about war and wanted to be in the army when he grew up. His questions and general conversation became so inappropriate and uncontrollable that finally, when he was 11, the school hired a teacher to work with just two or three incorrigible children and he was one of them. Of course, it didn't work. The three fed off each other and one day James came to school with a large knife. That was his last day that year at the public school.

I had been involved with James since he was in kindergarten, but I had never been his teacher. I was given that task after the knife incident. The bus brought him by himself, with an aide, to a city building away from the school and he and I worked in a huge, drafty empty room for one hour each morning. At the starting point, he couldn't write more than a couple of sentences, could do simple addition but no subtraction, and could read at a beginning first grade level, but his ability was much, much higher. By the end of the school year he read at fourth grade level, could add and subtract multi-digits and knew how to use a calculator to multiply and divide. He was able to write stories that filled a page.

I rode the bus home with him each day and we became the best of friends. How? I was the first person to answer those questions. It is as simple as that. He worked in very short spurts and received answers. He became calm and respectful. He still had big problems, but the improvement was amazing. Here's a little sample.

James: "How many bullets are in a bomb?"

Barb: "Here's your calculator. This first problem is easy. Get the answer written while I think about how many bullets are in a bomb. By the way, do you mean a little or a big bomb?"

James: "A BIG bomb!"

Barb: (touching the calculator), "Okay, I'm thinking while you work."

He hurriedly calculated the answer and wrote it down, looking at me expectantly.

Barb: "362 bullets, for a big bomb. Let me think about the little bomb while you do the next problem."

And so on.

I answered, calmly, with ridiculously phony information, just about every question he came up with, but I tried to reroute the questions to get them to be more appropriate. For example:

James: " How far away can you see an atom bomb? How many people will die?"

Barb: "This is a hard question. You write your next sentence in your story telling me what happened next while I think about it."

After he wrote the next sentence, I had him read it to me and we talked about what might be the next sentence, but then I said:

Barb: "Your question about atom bombs made me remember something you will want to know. In the 1940's there was a war and some very smart scientists were trying to figure out a powerful bomb and they finally did. It was the atom bomb. They hoped they wouldn't have to use it, but they did and it ended that war. That was World War II. Have you heard of it? Remember how you wondered how far away you could see it and how many people died? Well, I am going to bring a book tomorrow and you can find out exactly what the answer is. Let's both guess and see how close we are to the right answer. I think you can see it for 10 miles and that 1000 people died. What do you think?" Most of the time, I never knew the actual answers to his questions. I just knew he needed to **not** be dismissed.

I tried to start making the answers real and the questions more sensible and not so sensational, but at no time did I ever show shock at the questions. I tried to turn them into something educational. He felt less frantic, more respected, and calmer. If he swore, I didn't get angry, but I restated one of our main rules for our special classroom: If he swore, I couldn't answer until he said it again politely because it hurt my feelings to hear swearing. It sounds absurd, but it worked because I told him I really knew the answer and wanted to share it with him. In the beginning, I restated his question without the swearing, and he repeated it. Later, he willingly restated it.

I set up a points system for work completed and the reward was lunch at a restaurant of his choice with my husband as our guest. He knew my husband was a former Marine and he wanted to meet him since his interest was to become a soldier. When the lunch finally was earned, his first question for my husband was, "Did they let you hold an atom bomb". With a straight face, my husband said, "No. No one holds the bombs. They are very dangerous."

James had unbelievable problems, mostly caused from a sad lack of parenting and an even sadder lack of love and respect from anyone. His family really didn't care about him and his teachers couldn't handle him in the regular school setting. He needed a friend and someone who respected his inquiring mind. He needed to be loved and cared for and needed someone he could love. In our drafty, old empty room, that is what happened.

Summing It Up:

1. Do not ever, under any circumstance, consider any child "hopeless".
2. Look beyond the unlovable, and show love to every child.
3. Be creative. Be "unshockable." Be kind. Be respectful.
4. Control the learning environment. Be clever and do it in a way that works, which sometimes means starting where the student exists and moving in a better direction.

Chapter 10:

Jason

Later in my career I team taught with two fourth grade teachers, in a program that integrated mentally handicapped and regular ed students. It was in the first year of this experiment that I first taught Jason. He had Downs Syndrome, was fairly high functioning academically, and possessed very high social skills. Jason was impish, stubborn, and extremely popular, but he was a little thief. The regular education classroom wasn't set up in quite the "protected" way that my special classroom had been, and therein lay the problem. Each child had a tote tray drawer in his desk and Jason's would get stuffed so full it couldn't slide in. It was full of books, toys, teaching materials, and other things which didn't belong to him. One day a student was quite upset because her backpack was missing. The teacher automatically said, "Did you check Jason's tote tray?" How sad! He had developed a "rep" and it wasn't nice.

Jason excelled in almost all areas of his life. He was a fearless swimmer and could dive into the deep end of the pool by leaping up and spiraling down. He learned to skate and ride a bike during our community activities and made friends with the regular education students. He smiled through every activity and made each day fun for all of us. The "stealing" was constant but he never viewed it as stealing. He was very observant and realized quickly when he didn't have something that a fellow student had. For example, one day the jar of mealworms needed for the science lesson disappeared. Of course, you guessed it-the jar was in Jason's tote. We knew he wasn't a malicious thief because he never took sweaters or personal belongings of others. One day, Jason came late to school, and his fellow students were in the auditorium. I was working with a few other students when Jason came in. He walked to the door and looked in both directions. I asked what he was looking for and he said, "Where my kids?"

Jason's grandfather and his sister played the violin. At the beginning of our second year, the music teacher gave a talk to the school about the band and orchestra program and when she mentioned the violin, Jason jumped up and raised his hand. From that minute, he was determined to join the orchestra program and learn to play the violin. No mentally handicapped child had ever been in that program in our school, but I felt he was motivated enough to learn. The orchestra teacher accepted him with no hesitation. During the year, I went with Jason to each class and he learned to play "Twinkle Twinkle Little Star." Jason was so careful with his violin. Other students approached him with high 5's. His work ethic and pride in his accomplishment impressed everyone. There were two concerts during the year and he played with the group by staying with the basic rhythm, if not the actual notes, of the more difficult songs. His proud smile told the story. He was so happy and so were his parents, siblings, and grandfather.

Summing It Up:

1. Motivation is the key to success. Listen to children. Each child can be motivated by something you would never have imagined. Use it!

2. If children do something unacceptable, try to see what the reason might be before you automatically assume the worst.

3. Just because a child might not be capable of learning a skill completely, be aware that partial skill learning may play a positive role in his life.

Chapter 11:

Tommy

Near the end of a school year, I got a call from the teacher of the primary program asking me to come observe a little boy who would be coming to my intermediate special education program in the fall. My students were fully integrated into two fifth grade classrooms and she was worried that he wouldn't fit in. When I observed him, I saw a smiling, non-verbal unkempt whirling dervish who pinched, hit, scratched, grabbed, and spit on anyone who came close; therefore, the staff kept him isolated. His desk was at least 10 feet behind the other desks and an aide was sitting right with Tommy. His teacher explained to me, quite sweetly actually, that he was incorrigible. Although she had tried hard with him, he was impossible and she felt certain he couldn't survive in my integrated classroom setting. She wanted to send him to a district program for students who simply couldn't be controlled. The ratio was top heavy with adults and the students had very limited access to the real world. As I watched him, I saw no love from anyone; I saw no "like" either. I saw irritation, disgust, and downright dislike from the aide.

I also saw a lot of intelligence in Tommy. He was controlling his little isolated world as well as he could, and I could see that he was enjoying tormenting the aide and anyone else who came near him. At the end of the observation, his teacher asked, "Do you see what I mean that he won't fit into your group?" I answered, "No. I want him." And, I got him!

Our classroom was set up with six desks pushed together to form groupings. Each set of six had five regular ed students and one of my students. The fifth grade teacher and I decided to put Tommy's desk in a group of well-behaved kids. The boy directly opposite Tommy was Carl, a very nice red head, who, despite having his hair pulled, his arm scratched, and his clothing grabbed frequently by Tommy, instantly bonded with him. Instead of getting angry, Carl picked up the cues from us and handled Tommy with amazing skill. One of us was always very near Tommy, and when he grabbed, hit, scratched, or pulled hair, we instantly put our hands in our own lap and said, "Hands in your lap, Tommy!" and he'd copy our example. He had no language at all and these aggressive acts were actually his attempt to get attention. Soon we were able to say, "Where do your hands go?" and he would stop the behavior and put his hands in his lap.

Day by day, Tommy improved, with a few steps back and a few more forward. All the while, Carl remained his buddy and seemed oblivious to pain. After Tommy put his hands in his lap, we would say, "Let's try this again" and whatever was happening when the aggressive act occurred would be repeated without the aggression. For example, if we were lining up to leave the classroom and Tommy grabbed at the child next to him, we'd say, "Where do your hands go, Tommy?" and then we'd say, "Let's try lining up again with hands down." We'd take Tommy back to his desk, call him up to the line, and demonstrate "hands down." It was a slow process, but very successful.

One day, a staff member walked into our door and as she passed Tommy, he reached out and grabbed her skirt. She was shocked, but even more surprised, as were we, when Carl immediately said to her, "Let's try that again. Will you please go out and come in again so Tommy can show you how he keeps his hands down?" And the teacher walked back outside and re-entered! Tommy kept his hands down and Carl gave him a high 5 and then hugged him.

Tommy's big desire was to be part of the group and be accepted. He got more than that from Carl. He got real friendship and love. And Carl? He got the inspiration for his future career as a special ed teacher!

Summing It Up:

1. Accept every child. Demonstrate your acceptance every minute of every single day. Children can tell if you don't like them or one of their classmates.

2. Acts of aggression have a reason. You have to figure out that reason and help the child find a new way to cope. In Tommy's case, his aggressiveness started because he couldn't communicate. With a concentration on teaching him to use sign language, his need for aggression diminished.

3. Children learn from other children. Foster this and use it to help you teach.

4. Promote and value kindness and a community of acceptance for all people in your classroom.

Chapter 12:

William

William was a big, soft 11-year-old who was brilliant, but socially inept. He was at the high end of the autism spectrum and knew a lot of irrelevant disconnected information. His parents brought him in on the first day of school and informed me that, although he was in this school for the mentally handicapped, he certainly was not retarded. They also gave me the rules that he was never, ever to be photographed for a newspaper article and his name was never to be made public. As they were telling me this, William started crying pitifully, put his hands up and started flailing, running in circles, and crying louder and louder and screeching in a very high voice, "Go AWAY, fly!" "Go AWAY, fly!" We all turned to see what on earth was wrong and we saw a fly casually buzzing near William, and in a very cruel twist of fate, actually began following him.

His mom and dad said, "Oh, by the way, he's terrified of flies."

The fly phobia was intense and very disruptive. If a fly flew into the classroom, William became hysterical. He cried, screamed, put his hands on his ears, and begged for help. One day, he was so upset he ran from the classroom. Another time, when we were on a field trip, a fly came into the van and he almost opened the door to get out at 35 miles per hour. I had to do something.

I started collecting flies in a jar and kept it in the classroom in an attempt to desensitize William. We talked to the flies and acted like they were class pets. Bizarre? Yes! One day, my aide, Irene, actually stunned a fly, but didn't quite kill it and she perched it, like a bird on her finger and walked from student to student asking each child to say hello to her "pet fly." She called it Buzzy and by the time she got to William, she was truly attached to the fly!

"William, say hello to my friend," she said.

William screeched, "Kill it, Barb! Kill it, Barb!" and flailed his arms, smacking the groggy fly and finishing the poor thing off.

Irene was beside herself, because by that point she had convinced herself that he really *was* her pet! "William! You killed my fly!" I thought she'd cry and William actually did cry. My classroom had become nuts and I was ready to cry, too.

The point of this is to let you know that sometimes a teacher gets an idea, tries it and it doesn't work. That's okay. You will constantly be tweaking your plans and making sure they do eventually work.

Once I realized that William was not going to befriend any flies, I decided to try something else. He was frightened and couldn't concentrate on anything if a fly came into the classroom so I decided to put him on fly control on our list of classroom jobs. I put a rolled newspaper on his desk and if he spotted a fly, it was his job to let me know and I immediately took the paper and killed it. It was fascinating to see how putting William in control calmed him down. I still remember teaching and suddenly hearing, "Barb! THERE'S A FLY!" and I would stop teaching, walk over to his desk, get the paper, and smack that fly. The children clapped and William would say, "HE'S A GONER, BARB!"

Summing It Up:

1. If a behavior is so intense that a student can't learn and you can't teach, you have to devise a plan to deal with it. Sometimes the solution seems ridiculous, but it might work. If not, go back to the drawing board.
2. If a student is afraid, he can't learn. You have to help him be in control of his fear.
3. Never be afraid or embarrassed to change your plan. You should constantly be assessing what you are doing, monitoring its effectiveness, and making changes to ensure success.

Chapter 13:

F.J.

Everyone loved F.J. When I met him he was a very sad, depressed fifth grader whose dad was unknown and whose mom was in jail for drugs. He and his little brother were living in a foster home and F.J. hated it. He wanted to have his mother come home and he would take care of her. If she came home, he knew that she would want to stay away from drugs because she loved him and they could live happily ever after. He was such a bright child and so interested in amazing facts about animals, the planets, the stars, and many other subjects. He was interested and so interesting. I was not ever his teacher, but was a resource for his teachers and I set myself up as a friend to F.J. Our friendship lasted for three school years, and I'm still amazed at his journey.

One day I was called to try to help F.J. who was sitting in the quad and refusing to return to class. I walked slowly over to him and sat down on the bench next to him as if I had all day to visit and bask in the sunshine. When I asked him what he was upset about, he didn't hesitate. "I'm through with school. I'm in trouble because I'm not ever going back to my foster home."

"What can I do to help you, F.J.?"

"Go get Randy [his 1ˢᵗ grade brother] because I'm taking him with me."

"Where are you going to live?" I asked with a tone that said that a 10-year-old and a 6-year-old could choose to live alone.

"I'll find a cave in those mountains right there," he said, pointing to the mountain range behind the school, "and I'll eat leaves." Suddenly, he jumped up, grabbed a large leaf from the tree we were under, and ate it! I stayed calm but I was worried that it might be poisonous. He knew it was a strange thing to do, so he started to walk away from the campus. I walked with him.

I asked him if something had happened at the foster home to cause him to be upset. He was so matter-of-fact, telling me that it was clear to him that they intended to keep him away from his mother forever and he wasn't going to put up with that. I knew there had to have been a catalyst and finally he said, "Margie [his foster mother] told me I had to feed the chickens and I didn't want to. She told me that she knew my mother hadn't made me do chores, but I had to do chores at her house. She hates my mom and I hate Margie. She's mean."

I knew it was hopeless to tell him he had to go back to the home, and he was refusing to go back to class, so I said, "I am going to help you, F.J. I'm going to tell you how to handle this, okay? "He agreed to listen and sat on the ground. I wasn't really thrilled with sitting on the ground, but I plopped right down beside him. "Let's call Esther, your social worker, and tell her your side of this story and see what she can do. She might be able to let you know if there are any other good choices for you and Randy. I know you trust her. I'll stay with you until she comes. Shall we do that?" He agreed.

I called Esther on my cell phone and she was at our school within an hour. I told her to meet us in the library. While we waited, F.J. began talking about the solar system and how he'd like to fly to another planet. We looked up books on the subject and read until Esther came.

By the end of the day, F.J. agreed to go back to Margie's house until Esther arranged a new placement. She hadn't felt the match was a good one anyway, so she didn't fight the change at all. F.J. felt listened to. He was placed in a home in a nearby city for the rest of the school year.

At the beginning of the next year, I was told that F.J. was at the middle school, back in our district. I was anxious to see him and to find out how everything had gone for him. He was 11, in sixth grade, but he seemed to have matured about 10 years. I took him out of class for a few minutes and, with a profoundly sad face, he told me his story. His mother had been released from her jail sentence, had come home, and he and his brother were able to visit her regularly. His hope was that they would be able to live together and be a family again. He told me that he was so happy and he was positive that she loved him and his brother enough to never take drugs and never go to jail again. In a quiet monotone he said, "But she didn't love us. She was arrested again and now she'll be in jail for a long, long time." There was nothing about F.J.'s face that was childlike.

F.J. had a male teacher that year that made all the difference for him. Mr. James showed so much respect for F.J.'s mind and made himself available so that F.J. had someone to trust and to talk to. During that school year, we were astounded at the progress he made, mostly in his acceptance of his fate. He had given up on his mother and slowly realized he had to move on. He became fiercely protective of his brother. Mr. James has stayed in contact with F.J. from that day until now. I talked to him a couple of years ago and learned that both F.J. and Randy had been adopted by a couple in Florida and seemed very content. He still calls Mr. James a few times each year. He made a decision to move on, and he did it.

Summing It Up:

1. All children need to be heard. The stranger their conversation, the more carefully you need to listen.
2. If a child is in foster placement, try to find out the pertinent information about his placement, his case manager, and as much about his history as possible. It will help you help him.
3. Understand that children love their parents, even when their parents are unlovable in your eyes. Respect their feelings, but guide them to safe decisions.
4. Be aware that you will have students occasionally who have had experiences you can't imagine. Don't prejudge them. Give them the tools to help them and the support of a caring adult.

Chapter 14:

Michelle

Michelle was born with spina bifida but she was able to walk with braces on her legs. It was amazing that she could walk, but after I had known her for a brief time, I realized how determined she was to be independent. She wanted to be exactly like the typical children of her age.

She came to me when she was 9 from a program for higher functioning special ed students because of her lack of progress. She fascinated me because anyone talking with her would never suspect her learning difficulties. She tried so hard but she made very slow progress. She was age appropriate in her interests, actions, and activities but she struggled to retain academic information. She was only in my class for a couple of months when summer vacation started. I was tutoring students and when her parents asked if I might tutor Michelle that summer, I jumped at the chance to try to figure out this puzzle.

Directionality was a major problem for Michelle. I was trying to teach her to write her first name in cursive. She knew right from left, but if told to draw a line toward the right, she would often draw it to the left, or down, or up. It was hit and miss. I used a light colored marker for her to trace the direction of parts of the letters. She could trace on the line, but even tracing the thick marker line was difficult because her pencil line wobbled above or below as she struggled to follow the line. Once she mastered the tracing, she worked on forming the letters with an example and verbal cues and by following my pencil as I wrote each letter above where she was writing. The letter that was most difficult was the "c." As her pencil moved from the "i" to the top of the "c," she invariably made her pencil turn left, or back toward the "i" instead of right. I modeled simultaneously with my pencil and gave the verbal cues of "right," without success.

There have been so many times during my career that a child got stuck at a certain level of a skill and I tried many different ways to help him get "unstuck," but Michelle's problem was very difficult to solve. Week after week we worked diligently on writing her name and the "c" needed help every time. The day of our breakthrough is one I will always remember because it was so simple and so successful. I was sitting across from her and we were both close to the wall by the table. As she finished the "i" and started up to write the "c," her hand, as usual, started veering back to the left and I tapped the wall to her right and said "This way, Michelle." Her hand immediately turned toward the sound of my tapping. We tried it over and over and when I tapped the wall, her hand followed; when I didn't tap the wall, her hand turned back.

After experimenting with tying her directionality to sound, I realized how perfect the relationship was. She was soon able to write her first name in cursive with no problem if I gave a simple tap as she started the "c". I said "to the right" each time I tapped and eventually I was able to say "to the right" as I lifted my hand as if to tap. I faded the cues and soon she could write her name without any cues at all. I used this technique of guiding her motions toward sound in other examples as time went by. It was so interesting and so randomly discovered and so helpful. It reinforced that each individual child has his own learning style and how important it is for teachers to discover that style.

Summing It Up:

1. Some children learn best visually, some learn auditorily, some tactilely, or some through a combination of one or more. It is your challenge to discover what works best for each child you teach. Sometimes that is very difficult. Experiment. Don't be satisfied with trying the same approach with all of the children in your classroom. Striving for the middle ground or majority is unfair to those learners who need a special technique.

2. If a child is learning a new skill and is making no real progress, break the skill into smaller sequential steps. Be creative.

3. Once you have provided your student with a "crutch" to facilitate learning a difficult skill, be certain to plan an exit strategy by fading the help in a logical way to prevent loss of the skill.

Chapter 15:

Michael

After my first retirement, I was hired by a district to give suggestions to improve the special education classes. One day as I was observing in the resource class, I noticed Michael. The class was split into two separate groups, one doing spelling and one having reading instruction. Unfortunately, for Michael, the reading instruction was over his head. The level was about second grade and he couldn't read many of the words and was visibly miserable. When called on, he hung his head and mumbled, guessing at the words and speaking so softly no one could really hear him. I observed for several days, and I saw many students who were breezing through the level and many who were struggling. One of the changes I implemented very quickly was to individualize the instruction in that resource program, but it was too late for Michael. He informed his fifth grade teacher that he wouldn't go back to Resource. Mr. Barron tried talking, cajoling, and even bribing Michael, but to no avail. I looked up Michael's testing results and he was basically at a kindergarten level in reading. He had a severe learning disability but a normal IQ. At 11, he was done. He hated school, hated reading, hated the resource class, and I'm afraid he hated himself. I was intrigued.

I called Michael into my office and in a very business-like voice, said, "Michael, I brought you in here to ask you if you would like to stop going to Resource."

I seemed so agreeable about it that he looked up in surprise and said, "I'm not going back. I told my mom already and I'm not going back. I can read okay. I don't need to go. I don't like it. I want to stay in my room." He might have gone on and on, but I stopped him by agreeing with most of his points.

I said, "I agree with you and I want you to stay in your class, but Mr. Barron and I both feel that you actually want to read better so, after watching you in Resource for awhile, I found the perfect reading program for you. He wants you to come over here to my office for just 10 minutes each day. You won't miss any of the class work time. You'll come during the silent reading time after lunch. What do you say?"

His attitude and lack of self confidence brought about a quick, "I don't want to."

I responded, "What would you say if I told you that in one school week you will be able to read a story by yourself?" He looked up and his expression told me that he absolutely knew that wasn't true. I knew it was, though, so I said, "I'll make a deal with you, Michael. If you will come over here and work in my office for 10 minutes each day this week, just the two of us, no other kids around us, I **promise** you will read a story by yourself. If you can't, you don't have to come anymore. Mr. Barron is hoping you will come."

The program I used was the Edmark Sight Reading Program which I had used with many students with mental retardation, but Michael was not mentally handicapped. I had also used it when tutoring intermediate or middle school aged students who had given up on themselves and their ability to read. It isn't babyish and words are learned so quickly that the child gets an immediate boost in morale. The first three words, *horse, A*, and *yellow* can form an instant phrase. The program has little booklets that make up sentences and simple stories using the first few words. Michael learned five words the first day, read phrases, matched pictures to words and, although he was shy and didn't smile, he worked hard. I gave him cards with his words to take back to class to show his teacher. The second day, he was a few minutes early, learned ten more words, did several lessons matching phrases, pictures, etc. He seemed surprised at how easily he was learning to read. At the end of the second day, I gave him worksheets using the first 15 words, stapled together with a cover on the front with "Homework" written on it. I asked him to do the sheets at home and bring them back the next day. When he left, he smiled. On the third day, he almost bounced into my office, handed me his homework packet, and told me he read all of it to his mom.

"She must have been very proud of you, Michael, because you are learning so fast." He smiled again. At the end of the third day Michael asked me for more homework. We covered many words over the next two days and Michael was happy to find out that he actually knew some of the words in the program allowing us to cover more words that he didn't know. On Friday, Michael came in and I gave him a set of booklets covering the words he had learned so far. He read them easily and was amazed at himself. He learned about 25 words that first week, but what he learned that was much more important, was that he **could** learn to read. He had given up and now he was back in the game.

When using this program to jumpstart a student, I usually move pretty rapidly into a little more typical program. In the third week of our lessons, Michael graduated into a pre-primer program. I told him that if his teacher agreed, I would like to have him come for 30 minutes so we could move along faster. His response?" I could come for an hour if you want me to!" There is absolutely nothing more motivating than success!

I used a program that was about a pig and a boy and the pictures were realistic. He moved from being a kindergarten level reader to a second grade reading level in a little less than one semester of one-on-one daily tutoring. He was at fourth grade reading in vocabulary and comprehension by the end of the school year. He was a perfect example of the power of individualization, kindness, and privacy. He ended fifth grade able to hold his own in his classroom, with self-confidence and pride.

At the end of the school year, Michael's mother asked for a conference with me. When she talked to me, she cried. She told me that she knew he wasn't "stupid", but he was convinced that he was. She was so emotional about her son and so proud of him. She told me that he brought home the papers I gave him each day and wanted to read to her. She asked me if I could give her some materials to help him continue improvement over the summer. Of course, I was happy to develop a summer packet for Michael and his mother. When she left my office, it was my turn to smile!

Summing It Up:

1. When a child thinks that he is a failure, he probably will be, unless you intervene.
2. If a child gives up on himself, he will resist learning, will be depressed and defensive. You have to prevent him from giving up.
3. Include a struggling child in the solution to his problem.
4. Be aware of many programs, techniques, and strategies so that you can find the perfect one to assure a level of immediate success, to help a child start to turn his or her attitude from negative to positive.

5. Be prepared to make the most appropriate materials, if none can be found, to raise a child's self- image.

6. Teaching children at a level that is above their current skill level will often lead to discouragement. Avoid it. Don't be a lazy teacher. Find the best materials.

Chapter 16:

Margie

Margie! Margie! Margie! What will you say next? We never knew. Margie didn't take any time at all to become known by literally every child at our elementary school. She was the most social child I've ever taught.

She was 9 when I met her on the first day of school. Her mom told me that she was a very friendly, talkative girl but was a little bit too social and might bother other children. About that time, approximately five minutes after entering the class, Margie had already hugged each of the other students in the room and had taken the hand of Ray, a particularly shy little boy and was headed for the toy shelf. Her mom started to say something to her and Margie started laughing and said, "Go home, Mom! Go home, Mom! I go on the bus!" while she gently pushed her mom toward the door.

As her mom exited, she looked back and said, "She loves school. You'll have to throw her out to get rid of her! And, oh, by the way, she's not toilet-trained." Four years later, Margie was selected to receive the Humanitarian Award given to a sixth grader each year. She well deserved it.

I taught Margie for four years of non-stop fun. She was concerned about everyone and everything except her bodily functions! She was totally unconcerned if she had bathroom accidents and no matter what programs I set up, we made no real headway. Although she was mentally handicapped, she was 9 and I knew she was capable of being trained. After a conference with her mom to find out how she was dealing with it at home, I discovered she wasn't having any better luck than I. I also found out that at 4:00, shortly after the bus ride home, Margie watched her favorite show on TV. We set up a special sticker card at school on which Margie would get a sticker if she arrived at school clean and dry which earned her morning recess time. The next block of time was between recess time and lunch. If she earned that "cleanliness" sticker, she earned lunch recess. She needed to stay clean after lunch until dismissal and if she earned that sticker, and was still clean when she arrived home she earned the right to watch her TV show at 4:00. Her mom expanded it to one more sticker at home between bus arrival and dinner. That sticker earned her the right to have dessert. By making this a school-home continuity program, Margie was toilet-trained 100% within a month. The key was that she didn't care, but we set up rewards that were important to her.

At our first home visit, I asked Margie's parents if they had any problems at home that I might be able to help. Their main frustration was that Margie was terrified of flying in an airplane, or even being in an airport. They had moved here from Kentucky, where all the grandparents, aunts, and uncles still lived. It was difficult to travel back to see them because they could never fly. I decided to try to help. Every Thursday was our community functioning day so I decided to start each trip for awhile at the airport. We began by just driving to the airport, parking on the second level parking garage, which was open air, and we watched planes take off for a few minutes.

The first time we went Margie was frightened by the planes. She cried while she kept her hands over her ears. All of the other children were thrilled by the planes. After about three weeks, Margie stopped holding her ears and stopped crying. For the next few weeks, we walked into the airport and got ice cream cones. She loved ice cream, so that went pretty well, but she kept saying, "Let's go, Barb. I HATE airplanes! Let's go, Barb. I HATE airplanes! Let's go, Barb. I HATE airplanes!" She did manage to eat the ice cream between her protests.

Then it was time for the next big step, so we went through the metal detectors and walked to a gate. This was before the rules at airports changed. Everyone chose a seat and we watched planes through the big glass windows. Finally, after about ten weeks of this desensitizing, I got special permission to take Margie on board a plane. *Disaster* is the only word for the first time we did this. She started whimpering as I walked down the jet way, but it turned into full blown screaming by the time we got to the door. The pilot met us at the door, got down to her level and gave her a pair of wings. He had been warned about her fear. We did this three times before we were able to get her on the plane and in a seat, at which point she reached into the seat pocket in front of her and started looking at the magazine pictures. Margie and her family are able to fly now.

Everyone knew Margie because she didn't have a shy bone in her body and was unbelievably aware of every little bruise, cut, red mark on everyone. I've seen her dash over to a fifth grade boy on the playground, grab his arm where an adhesive bandage was, and kiss it, saying, "Mikie! What happened? Are you sick, Mikie? I love you, Mikie!"

The amazing thing was that Mike said, "It's okay, Margie. It's just a little sore," and then go on with whatever he was doing. There was just something about her genuine concern that kept those intermediate aged kids from getting embarrassed or upset with her.

During the third and fourth years that I taught her, I team-taught with two regular education teachers, meshing our students in an experimental integration program. Margie was a very popular child and was invited to a fifth grade girl's birthday party along with only ten other girls. It was definitely a high point. We saw so often how the general ed kids accepted her even though it would seem that she would embarrass them. One day, a boy raised his hand and asked if he could go to the restroom. Margie said, in her sweet, loud, voice, "Greg! Do you have to pee, Greg?" When he returned, she called out, "Good Boy, Greg! You get your sticker, Greg!" He smiled and said, "Yea, I get my sticker, Margie." I was always so surprised at how 10-year-old boys didn't tease each other when she said these things. I believe it was because Margie was genuine in her comments and concerns.

Even Mrs. McNulty, the general ed teacher in Margie's class accepted what she did and said. Margie always called her "Nulty." She'd call out, "Nulty, I need help!"

Every time, Mrs. McNulty would say, "Margie, my name is MRS. MAC Nulty," accentuating those parts of her name. After quite a long time, Margie started calling her "MAC."

We'd hear, "MAC, I need help!"

Mrs. McNulty would respond, "What's my whole name, Margie?"

Margie's response would usually be, "MRS. MAC." You would think poor Mrs. McNulty would have given up, but she didn't. In our last year with her, Margie finally got it right! She was assigned to a small science group working on a measurement project. She saw Mrs. McNulty helping another group, so she jumped up and went over to the child Mrs. McNulty was helping, threw her arms around the child, and said, "I love her, Mrs. McNulty!" Ignoring the inappropriateness of Margie's actions, Mrs. McNulty was so thrilled that she stopped the whole class to report the big news that Margie finally got her name right. There was just something about Margie that made everyone happy.

One of Margie's favorite friends was named Billy. Our integrated program meshed my mentally challenged children with fifth graders, so on the first day of the new school year, when Billy was going to be in sixth grade, Margie saw him walking with his new class and she just stepped out of our line, ran up to him, took his hand and went right into his new class with him. Of course, I went right after her but just couldn't help appreciating how special their relationship was when this sixth grade boy, in front of all the kids in his new class, gave her a hug and told her she needed to go back to her class and he would see her later. No embarrassment, no shyness, no hurtful comments to Margie from Billy-just a genuine hug for a genuine friend.

Summing It Up:

1. Celebrate the unique qualities of each student.
2. Work closely with parents. Home visits are a great source of information for you and the parents. They can set the tone for success.
3. Listen to the concerns of parents. Perhaps you can help solve problems for them.
4. Encourage a feeling of family and community in your classroom. It should be the same type of safe haven that a home should be.

Chapter 17:

Mel

Mel was in my class of mentally handicapped students but when he was in his neighborhood, or away from the school, no one would ever know he had any problem at all. He seemed completely normal. I watched him help others, draw pictures of airplanes and trucks, and speak of topics interesting to any seventh grade boy.

I preferred not to read the comments from prior teachers until after I had met my new students, so I was amazed by Mel. He seemed totally out of place. The first day of school in a class of this type can be wild because of the nature of some of the handicaps, so it was just natural that I enlisted Mel's help at every turn that day. "Mel, please give me that red towel," and he gave it to me. "Mel, I need four blocks" and he gave them to me. Yet when I asked Mel what time it was, he had no idea. When I asked what color his shirt was (and it was red), he had no idea. When I asked him to tell me what number was on the door (it was 4) he couldn't name it. So I sat with Mel and started testing him on basic sight words and he couldn't read any at all, not one single word, not even the word "a." Now this was an interesting kid!

Mel had a severe learning disability and had no success at the labeling level, but he had a clear comprehension of numbers, letters,

93

colors, shapes, and words. You may remember Donald (Chapter 7), who had similar difficulties. Remembering that I hit upon the power of association with Donald gave me a starting place with Mel. Mel was a junior high student and his skill needs were higher than Donald's so I ended up finding a variety of answers for him.

We tackled colors and shapes, and he learned them quickly through association. Like Donald, if he saw blue, he learned to say "blue sky." Red was "red fire." White was "white snow." This was possible because he knew that the sky is blue, fire is red, and snow is white, so by assigning the cue word to the color card and then having him repeat the two words together, he made the association including the physical look of the color. In the beginning, I'd show him the blue card, point up and say "sky blue" and soon all I had to say was "sky" and he'd say "blue", and quite quickly he jumped from the sight of the card to saying "sky blue" and then just "blue". We used this association technique with the basic shapes as well.

Mel could count by rote very easily so I taught him to name the numerals by teaching him to start counting the clock numerals beginning with the number 1 until he came to the matching number he was shown. This worked for the numerals 1-12. Later, he carried a card with 1-100 on it and he found the numeral on it and counted to name it. Awkward? Clumsy? Time-consuming? Definitely, but it was a method that worked for him. He learned to put value on the numbers by counting out objects until he came to the number named. He used this technique to add in this way:

$$4 + 5 =$$

Step 1: Locate the 4 on a clock or watch. Start with number 1 and count to be able to name the 4. Draw lines next to the 4 counting until he ended up with 4. Do the same for the 5. Count all of the lines (9). Once he said "nine," he began counting around the clock until he said the word "nine" and he copied the look of the number as his answer. Yes, very awkward. We did this to help him understand the process, but we quickly taught him to use a calculator. He could give meaning to the calculator answer by using pennies or small objects to count out the amount.

I decided to skip teaching him to label the alphabet letters and went straight to teaching him a combination of simple sight words from the Edmark Sight Reading Program and consonant sounds. The Edmark program uses matching words as part of the program. Mel was expert at matching. I enhanced this program by placing a picture with each word on separate cards. The first word in the program is *horse* so, initially, I put a picture of a horse next to the word *horse*, a picture of a car next to the word *car,* and so one. Otherwise, I followed the program lessons and gradually changed the word cards so that only the word was on the front and the picture was on the back. Slowly but surely he learned many words without looking at the picture.

Simultaneously, I worked on the initial consonant sounds in an incidental way. I discovered that if I said, "What sound is the letter b?" Mel could give the sound, but if I showed him a written letter "b" and asked for the sound, he couldn't give it. I began with the verbal only, then combined verbal and written, and finally was able to eliminate the verbal cue. After discovering the best way to have some reading success, I spent most of my time with him on community words such as restroom signs.

Mel moved after one year in my class so I don't know how he did later in life. He probably became successful and independent working in a job that did not require much reading. He understood clearly that he had to compensate and through that understanding he worked hard and let me help him. I hope he kept that attitude. The phrase, "thinking outside of the box" applied to the techniques I had to try to develop for Mel.

Summing It Up:

1. Try to remember special techniques and tricks you used on other students who had similar learning issues. Try them and tweak them when necessary.

2. Be creative. Record what you are doing and the daily results so that you will be more in control. Being aware of progress or lack of progress helps you know when to monitor and adjust your instruction.

3. Help the student understand your plan. Stress his strengths to build his weaknesses.

4. Try to hone in on the most important skills for a particular student.

Chapter 18:

Shelly

Shelly had brain cancer when she was a baby. She was profoundly mentally handicapped and had a glass eye. She had no language at all and made very few sounds, but she seemed quite happy within herself. She never cried, never made a fuss, followed the group easily, played very quietly and alone, mostly playing with her own hands or feet. She was a child who could take last place for attention if a teacher weren't careful.

She was 7, quite isolated, but sweet and happy. About a week into the school year, my primary class was on the small playground and Shelly was in the sandbox, lifting up sand and letting it fall on her head. I walked over to try to redirect her to put the sand in a cup, but when I got close, I nearly fainted. Her glass eye was gone! I knew it had been in when we came outside, but it was certainly not in now. I called out to Jane, my aide, "Hurry! Help me! Shelly's eye is gone." We sifted through the sand and finally found the eye gazing up at us! The school nurse cleaned the eye and carefully put it in the socket, but to her surprise, she put it in backwards! The nurse and my aide dissolved into gales of laughter. When they brought Shelly to me, they tried to be professional, but some situations make that pretty difficult I would say that there was definitely more to Shelly than "met the eye" but that will come later.

Working with students with profound retardation can be very difficult. Progress is often very slow. The first step with Shelly was to watch her and try to read her. What interested her? Like most visually impaired children, her interests began with her own body. She played with her hands constantly and waved her arms in slow, methodical waves, and she liked the feel of her body on textures. Beyond that, it was obvious that she enjoyed music. She made singing sounds even without music in the background, but when she heard music, her attention shifted from herself to the sounds. Her head came up and her hands clapped or clasped and her torso swayed. The first good bit of information that helped me teach Shelly was that she had basic rhythm. She moved slowly to slow music and rocked to fast music.

My first and biggest job was deciding what was important for Shelly to learn that would help her have a productive life. I met with her parents to get some help. If you are teaching regular education students, the goals we set up for Shelly will seem very removed from what you are doing, but the most important lesson to learn is that each student has unique needs. Shelly's parents wanted her to come to their voices when called. They wanted her to be able to dress herself, put shoes on, and brush her teeth, and they wanted her to understand many basic commands and single step directions. They also hoped that someday, Shelly might speak.

All teaching should include frequent record keeping demonstrating progress or lack of it. Teachers need to modify instruction if progress is too slow. When teaching a student with as severe a handicap as Shelly had, it is especially critical to have daily recordings so that the teacher and parents can see the very slightest growth. Each of her goals had to be broken down into very small sequential steps and we had to decide exactly what the parents needed. Sometimes, a partial skill is a wonderful goal because it helps the child and the parent. In Shelly's case, we decided to start with teaching Shelly to help when an adult put a shirt on her. Her job was to be engaged in the process by lifting her arm when told and pushing her arm through the sleeve opening when told to push. Sounds simple, but It wasn't. Imagine, though, how much this would help her parents because they wouldn't have to pick up her arm and fight to get it in the sleeve opening and try to keep Shelly from walking away while they tried to put the shirt on her. We combined Shelly's love of sing song tones with our instructions about raising her arm and understanding the command "push" and it worked in time.

At first we sang, "Shelly, put your arm up, up, up, Shelly, put your arm UP, UP, UP. While we sang, we manipulated her arm and soon she put her arm up when we sang. Once we accomplished that consistently, we started teaching her to push her arm through the sleeve opening once we put her arm into it. With a fast, fun rhythm we sang, "Push, push, push it through, push, push, push it through *all through the sleeve!*" to the tune of the final lines of the song, "The Wheels on the Bus." A visitor coming into the classroom might have thought we were a bit strange, but it worked.

Shelly was the lowest functioning child I had worked with so everyday was a learning experience for me. But I have always treasured my two years with her. She taught me so much about individual differences and the need for individualization in the classroom. She also taught me about partial skill learning and about not wasting a child's time with unnecessary skills.

Shelly never learned to speak while I taught her and I don't think she ever did, but we made exciting headway in vocalization. We discovered that she could mimic some sounds and also could mimic broad body motions. She would generally use low sing-song sounds most of the time but occasionally she would squeal loudly. I came up with an experiment to respond to the louder squealing and come to her and "play" in some way, such as clapping her hands while I said, "Yes, Shelly, Here I am." I laughed and acted very outgoing and happy. Amazingly, after a few months of this immediate social reinforcement for her louder "calling", it became obvious that she understood how to use the squeal to call me. I almost cried the first day that I realized her squealing was purposeful. That day, I put a record on the record player and danced with her when we played.

Summing It Up:

1. Keep good, clear data. Record daily or weekly at a minimum.
2. Respect all students and teach meaningful information.
3. If you are a regular education teacher, you will undoubtedly have students with special needs participating in your room. Do not baby sit these children, or expect them to just try to work at a level they can't handle. Work with parents, or with the special education specialist to provide appropriate education. If the student is in your classroom, you need to be actively involved in his goal setting.
4. If you are given a challenge, face it head on, get all the help you can, and never forget that your one and only purpose is to **teach** every child in your care.

Chapter 19:

Joseph

Joseph was 5 and the most beautiful little boy I have ever taught. He looked completely normal, but was mentally handicapped and extremely hyperactive. He was absolutely never still. He came late into my special ed kindergarten program and changed it overnight. His parents didn't bring him in on his first day, probably out of fear that we wouldn't keep him.

He was totally wild. When the bus arrived and the driver opened the door, Joseph leapt from the top step to the sidewalk and I literally grabbed him in flight. I knew him from observations in his preschool program from the spring before so I was partly prepared, but my aide and I had several other 5 and 6-year-olds, including one very fragile little boy in a wheelchair. At one point that day, while trying to keep the children together I used a towel as a seatbelt to try to keep Joseph at the table. Suddenly, Joseph, with the chair strapped to his back, ran out of the classroom and out into the quad before my aide could catch him. After that, we called him "Mr. Turtle."

Hyperactive children can make a huge impact on your classroom, but Joseph made the typical hyperactive child look comatose. He was a tornado tearing through life, sparing nothing in his path. He didn't walk, he ran. He didn't hug, he mangled. He didn't giggle, he laughed hysterically. The child was unbelievable. I had only five students for the first week of school. They were calm, happy, well-behaved 5-year-old moderately mentally handicapped kids and in that first week I accomplished a lot of pre-testing.

Monday of the second week changed everything. Joseph arrived and nothing was ever the same. Someone had to be with him one-on-one. When we had the six children in one group for the morning opening, Cynthia, my aide sat behind his chair with one leg on either side of his chair. When we switched individual groups, Joseph was a group of one. We simply couldn't work individually with another child and give him one second's worth of independent work. When it was time to go into the play area, he couldn't be contained so I had to change all of the furniture around to create a play room closed off with shelving units on all four sides with a tiny opening for a doorway where my aide sat blocking the way of Joseph, the escape artist.

To say Joseph was enthusiastic and excited about everything would be a huge understatement. He literally bounced, twirled, and nearly flew from activity to activity. One day we were in a circle teaching the children a simple dance. I was behind Joseph holding both of his shoulders to keep him in his spot. My aide started the music, and Joseph made a vertical leap directly into my chin. My jaw hinge immediately became swollen and I couldn't close my mouth at all. Before school was out, the principal sent me to an orthodontist who gave me a cortisone injection into my jaw hinge. It instantly took the swelling down and I was able to close my mouth. I have had a semi-numb lower lip since that day.

I'm telling you about Joseph to illustrate the power of the technique of "re-do". Here's how it went with him. When the bus arrived in the morning, I was there. When he jumped from the top step to the sidewalk, I was ready, took him by the hand, and said, "Let's walk down the steps, Joseph." Then I took him up to the top and walked him down the bus steps. At that point, I greeted him with, "Good morning, Joseph. I'm so happy to see you. Let's find our classroom." I waited, holding his hand, until he stood calmly, and then we started to walk. He jolted ahead. As I turned back to our starting point, I said, "Let's **walk** to our classroom, Joseph." We continued this until he walked to the class holding my hand. As I was ready to open the door, I would say, "Put your backpack in your cubby. **Walk**!" When I opened the door and let go of his hand, he would begin to run, but I was ready! I got him back to the door, saying, "Remember, **walk**!" and walked most of the way to the cubbies holding his hand but then released him as I said, "**walk**." If he made it, that would be great. If he ran, back we'd "re-do." At the cubbies, he was told to "**walk** to your chair in the circle" and so on, through the day. In the beginning, my aide or I would spend most of the day with Joseph repeating the directions and the other would work with the rest of the children. This technique worked. By Christmas, Joseph was so much closer to becoming a student. I can't say he had arrived but he was closer.

I knew Joseph was capable of learning academically but I had to take care of school behaviors first before any other lessons could succeed. The first "reading" lesson was to understand the meaning of, "Put your hands in your lap." That was learned quickly, but the next step was for those hands to stay in his lap when I put a card or item on the table in front of him. We worked on color matching at first to try to teach the behavior of keeping his hands in his lap until asked to touch a particular colored item. I found out quite quickly what a huge mistake it was to use a colored block or three-dimensional object of any kind. They were simply too stimulating, so I used color cards.

At first, I had nothing on the table at all. I said, "Put your hands in your lap." Once that was done, I placed the card on the table in front of him and said, "Touch red," but as he lunged for it, it went sailing off the table. Time for a re-do, but I also modified this instruction by putting a little dollop of bulletin board putty on the back of each color card so that when I set it on the table in front of him and he "touched" it, it would stay put. The minute he touched the card, I would say, "Hands in lap." Of course, in the beginning, he grabbed the card and usually bent it up. By using a very calm voice, the re-do" technique, and a lot of patience, I taught Joseph to sit at the work table, put his hands in his lap and wait for an instruction, touch the item I asked him to touch, and then put his hands back in his lap. Miracle of miracles! You bet it worked and it really didn't take long. Calm consistency was the key.

I spent the entire school year teaching Joseph school behaviors, but I used colors, shapes, numbers, and letters simultaneously. The next goal after the "Hands in lap, touch, hands in lap" was to put two cards or items on the table and have him keep his hands in his lap, but look at each one as I pointed to it. I'd say as I pointed, "Look," then point to the other choice and say, "Look." As you can guess, it was extremely difficult for Joseph to keep his hands in his lap while he focused on one card or object at a time, but eventually, he did it. Before the year was over I was working on putting two cards on the table and showing Joseph a duplicate of one of them and asking him to match. All of this led to his ability to follow directions and focus and to become a reader-eventually!

Summing It Up:

1. Teaching school behaviors, class routines, and school rules are a requirement at the beginning of each school year. Some children require more of this than others. Take the time to teach what is needed because you can't get much done until you do.

2. Hyperactivity presents serious difficulties, impeding learning. You need to teach step-by-step procedures to give the child ways to learn in the classroom environment.

3. Find a way to teach each child, regardless of his problems. Whatever stands in the way of his or her success as a student needs to be worked through.

4. When one child seems to take an extra amount of time, analyze what needs to happen to get his school behaviors in line. Systematically teach the behaviors and record progress daily. For example, a student gets out of his desk too often, disrupting your lessons or disturbing others. He may also have ten other inappropriate behaviors, but in your opinion the one that is the **most** disruptive is the out-of-seat behavior, so that is the one you should record first. Set up a plan and be 100% consistent. Recording the daily data will keep you sane and will help you see progress. Once that behavior is under control, choose the next most disruptive behavior and start a program for it. You will see that each behavior will usually disappear faster than the one before.

Chapter 20:

Devon

Six year old Devon was one of the students I tutored in my retirement. The first day I went to his house I realized I had a major challenge ahead of me. He sat next to me and for a solid hour he talked almost non-stop. "Are you a teacher?"

"Yes," I said.

"Do you know how many teeth a shark has?"

"I'm not sure," I started to say and he got very upset and said, "YOU HAVE TO KNOW! YOU'RE A TEACHER! How many teeth does he have?"

"Quite a few, but let me show you something I have here," I said as I got out my color cards to test him.

"How many teeth?" The shark. How many teeth? Did you see one? How many teeth?"

After about five minutes of trying to change the topic, I realized it wasn't going to happen, so I said, "100 teeth!" It was a total guess. I hoped we could start the tutoring. Wrong!

"How do you blow up a shark? Do you use dynamite? Do you shoot it? How do you blow it up?"

"We need to start working now, Devon. Let's talk about sharks later, okay?" It wasn't okay.

The next seven years of tutoring went pretty much the same as this first lesson. Yet somehow, he and I both learned a lot about how to teach and how to learn and quite a bit about sharks!

Devon had Tourette's Syndrome and Autism. He had Attention Deficit/Hyperactive Disorder, was obsessive-compulsive, fearful, anti-social, and a discipline problem in his kindergarten class. He had petit mal seizures and medicine-caused hallucinations. He was in his second year of kindergarten and due to his inattentiveness he was still woefully behind in academic skills. It was obvious that he had normal intelligence, but it wasn't harnessed yet. His mother hired me four days a week, an hour each day, for seven years. He learned a great deal in reading, math, and writing during those seven years, but not at school. Year after year his teachers complained that he shouldn't be in their classrooms. Year after year he got into trouble for many inappropriate, often aggressive behaviors. Year after year his mother sent him to school but also paid me to teach him four hours a week. Those were the hours during which he learned. Devon's mother didn't want him to be in Special Education, which was too bad, but I have encountered this many times throughout my career. Eventually, he was part of Special Education, but his attitude about it was very poor, so he was serviced in his regular classroom. They did the best they could. I met with his teacher each year, and I tried to spend part of each hour on his homework.

I always had a plan when I walked into Devon's home, but I rarely was able to implement it as written. I learned the meaning of "monitor and adjust" during those years as never before. My goal and plan were clear in my mind and I creatively managed to accomplish the goal, but the plan often had to be scrapped. Here's an example of how a session went.

Barb: "Hi Devon, How are you today?"

Devon: "What's in your prize box?"

Barb: "It's your turn to answer first and then I will tell you what is in the prize box. How are you today?"

Devon: "Fine. What's in it? What's in it?"

Barb: "Something new is in the box and it has wheels." As I spoke, I put a sheet of lined paper in front of him. "What do you think it might be?"

Devon: "A car! "

Barb: "That's the title of our story today." I'd highlight the area in the center of the top line. "Write 'A Car' on the top line. That's your title."

Usually, at this point, he'd ask about 10 questions about the car, but I would just keep touching the highlighted area and telling him calmly to write the title, A Car. If he didn't, I'd print it on a card and hold it above where I wanted him to write, and I'd say, "Hurry and write your title because I want to show you the car." He would finally write it. By this point, I would have said the word "Title" about 15 times and he would know that is what he had written and would know it should be in the center of the top line.

I would then open the box and pull out the new car and say, "What color is this car, Devon?"

Devon: "Green! Why do you have a blue car? My car is gray. Your car is blue."

I would start writing the first sentence on a card. I'd highlight the spot where he should start his indented paragraph. "You write, 'The new car'." My plan now was for him to write this beginning and to come up with an ending to the sentence, but usually he'd become very distracted and change the subject completely.

Devon: "Are sharks in the Verde River?"

Barb: "Hey, I know that answer! Write '<u>The new car</u>' and I will tell you about the sharks." Finally, after several repetitions of this, Devon would quickly write the words, as I said, "You indented to start your paragraph. There are no sharks in the Verde River. Do you know why? I'll tell you when we finish this first indented sentence." After a few minutes, he'd finally finish the first sentence. I would have said the word "indented" several times. "There are no sharks in the Verde River because they live in salt water and the Verde is fresh water."

Our lessons were always like this. I had definite goals and I usually accomplished them, but how in the world he could retain any of it is a mystery. I used his obsessions about sharks, dinosaurs, horses, and even vampires to keep the lesson going. Sometimes, it took all week to accomplish the Monday goals and sometimes we buzzed through them. He was willing to do my work, although slowly and painstakingly, in order to discuss his interests with me. It certainly didn't go smoothly, but by the time he was ready for eighth grade he could write an essay; could add, subtract, multiply, divide, do fractions and decimals; could measure; and could read at about fourth to fifth grade level. Oh, and he knew a TON about sharks, dinosaurs, horses, and vampires!

Summing It Up:

1. Sometimes, a child with severe problems needs more than one teacher. Some children can't learn in a group setting.
2. Don't get irritated when a child's interests take precedence over yours. He's a child. Figure out a way to make your goals happen without denigrating his ideas.
3. Learn about various syndromes such as Tourette's, Autism, and Attention Deficit Hyperactive Disorder. Most, if not all, children with these syndromes will be in the general education

class. Also, learn about side-effects of medications your students might be taking.

4. If you are a general education teacher, be sure to become acquainted with the special education teachers in your school. Be mentors to each other.

Chapter 21:

Bonnie

Bonnie had cerebral palsy and was deaf and totally non-verbal. On the first day of school she came through the classroom door, stopped, looked around at the people, the shelves, the bulletin boards, and then noticed the desks with student names on them. Her mouth flew open, she inhaled and made the funniest noise, and moved as fast as she could from desk to desk until she found her name, sat quickly, and started touching each of the letters of her name with a love usually reserved for the most special thing a person could own. I was fascinated by her.

She was profoundly deaf, so whatever we had to say, or the noisy fun excitement in the room was of no interest, but that desk was a new and exciting world and, according to the name strip that said B-o-n-n-i-e, it was all hers.

I taught Bonnie for three years. She was in a class of mentally handicapped children located in the heart of an elementary school. She was very popular in the school even though she couldn't talk, drooled, and couldn't walk very well. What she had was personality with a capital P! She was not shy at all, engaged with other children appropriately, and demonstrated friendship and love. Sometimes we can all learn a huge lesson about human nature from a person like Bonnie.

Everyday was amazing with Bonnie. Our itinerant music teacher planned a listening game, but of course Bonnie couldn't hear the music at all. Each student had an instrument and when the music teacher played a tape of the sound of a simple instrument (drum, tambourine, flute, bells, or triangle), the child who had the instrument he heard on the tape stood up and briefly play his instrument. Bonnie had a tambourine and she watched while the teacher played the tape and the students played their instruments. She was so into the game but she was so profoundly deaf that she couldn't be hearing anything at all. Each time a child stood up to play, she smiled and got very excited. Finally, the music teacher played the sound of the tambourine and no child stood up. It took Bonnie about two seconds to realize that it must be her turn and she jumped up and played that tambourine with total enthusiasm. That demonstrated how completely Bonnie joined in, despite her hearing loss. She simply never would be left out of anything.

We worked on sign language with Bonnie. She needed a useful method of communication and she made fast progress. She learned the signs of pictured nouns and learned the signs used for communicating basic needs such as *eat, drink*, and *toilet*. but she didn't really seem to understand why we were working on the signs. One of the most exciting days in my teaching career came when we were doing a fun science activity with a general education fourth grade class. The children were constructing clay boats and trying them out in bowls of water to see if the boats would float. Bonnie was working with a little girl who was being very nice, but who had assumed that Bonnie couldn't really do the activity. Each girl had a piece of clay and Bonnie was trying to form a boat with her right hand. Her left hand was almost totally useless from the cerebral palsy. Her partner was experimenting with her own boat in the water and as she became more involved, she began to ignore Bonnie.

Pretty soon, Bonnie pulled on the bowl of water and signed "Bonnie". We had given her a name sign using the letter "b" on her chest. The fourth grader didn't understand at first, so Bonnie signed "Bonnie boat". I was so thrilled! Bonnie had actually realized the importance of signing and that its purpose was communication. She put that boat she had made into the water and it sank straight to the bottom. Bonnie thought that was pretty funny and her face lit up when her partner laughed. She took Bonnie's boat out of the water, turned up the sides, pointed at the water and told Bonnie to try again. Bonnie plopped it back in the water and it floated. She squealed and both girls laughed together.

Summing It Up:

1. The old cliché, "Don't judge a book by its cover" works with your students. Never assume a child can't participate or learn from an activity.

2. Children learn from each other. Having an opportunity to teach a peer is a powerful tool to use. Pairing strong and weak learners benefits both children.

Chapter 22:

Dan

Right after the New Year, every single year, we would get new students and it was usually because they were coming from another district program where they were failing. That can be a problem. According to his teacher, Dan was having difficulty learning to write his name, much less anything else, was struggling to learn to read, and was having a terrible time adding or subtracting, even with counters. He was in a higher level program for mentally handicapped students and they were sending him to my program for moderately mentally handicapped students. The teacher sent all his workbooks with him.

On the first day, I asked Danny, as he was called up 'til then, to write his name. He had a terrible time with the n's. He didn't know when to stop. He would write "Dannnny." I got out his reading book, sent by the teacher. He had no idea how to even begin. I put the book away in a drawer. I gave him a simple addition problem and some counters. I asked him what the top number was and he didn't know. I threw the test paper in the trash. Obviously, we needed to chuck what he was doing, and figure out where to start. For two years his old teacher had worked tirelessly on getting him to write "Danny." I told him he was a big boy now and we were changing it to "Dan." He could write it by 2 that afternoon, no problem.

Dan was a perfect example of how quickly a child can learn if you teach him where he is and not above his level. This is especially true for mentally handicapped students, but it applies to all children. Imagine trying to teach calculus to a first grader. Several years later, when that child is in high school, he will learn calculus as easily as he learned simple addition in first grade. Pre requisites are important. Dan was working in a published handwriting booklet, but needed to specifically work on the letters in his name. After immediately learning to write his first name, we worked on his last name. Once he accomplished that skill, we worked on the individual letters.

In math, he had been working on addition and subtraction, but couldn't even name numerals. He was able to count by rote to 100. We worked on naming numerals zero through 100, which he learned in about three weeks, and simultaneously, as he learned the name of a number, we worked on counting objects to equal the numbers. Once he had a clear ability to name numbers and match amounts to numbers, we started on simple addition. He came to us with that second grade reader but when I assessed his actual reading skills, he was at a beginning first grade level, which is where we began.

After I accurately assessed Dan's current skills and set up individualized instruction, he ended that school year ready to return to the higher level program. I found it really sad that he had to go through all of this switching around, changing friends, teachers, and schools. We had a meeting with his parents at the end of the school year and suggested he return to the higher program, but his parents did not want him to go back. It really wasn't right for him to stay in my program with children who were so far below his IQ, so we needed to compromise. The parents agreed to have him enrolled at a different school with a different teacher of the higher programming. Poor Dan. He was probably fine, but none of this hassle needed to occur.

Summing It Up:

1. Do your job! Assess your students carefully.
2. If you work on an objective with no improvement, reassess! Modify your instruction! Don't be a lazy teacher.
3. If your students are not succeeding, check all factors *including* yourself. Always be willing to look for better techniques and to listen to experienced mentors.

Chapter 23:

Freddy

Freddy, his older brother, and his mother were all autistic. They were part of a study about genetic autism. He was fascinating. His mother had a college degree but had difficulty parenting Freddy because she struggled with his same issues.

When she brought him into my special education kindergarten classroom on Back-to-School night when he was 5 he was holding a straw that he flexed in a precise pattern and his eyes never left it. His mom walked around the room looking at the bulletin boards and toys, but Freddy never saw any of it. He just kept flexing that straw. I was talking with other parents and children, but I couldn't help watching Freddy. He never stopped flexing!

Then as his mother casually passed a shelf with teaching materials on it, Freddy put the straw in his teeth, grabbed an open box with 1-inch colored cubes in it, dumped them out on the table next to the cabinet and quickly rearranged the box of cubes with all the colors together-all the reds, blues, yellows, greens and so on. He patted the blocks when they were perfect, held his straw again, and went back to flexing. Nothing I learned in college ever talked about straw-flexing, so what now?

I'll admit that the first month of that school year was one of the most difficult I've experienced because I just couldn't figure out what to do with Freddy. The year I had him was prior to the "autism explosion" we've experienced, so it was unusual for us to have autistic children in our classrooms. I met with Freddy's parents but it was difficult to get any help. Both of them had serious problems of their own. I asked his mother to be sure he didn't come to school with the straw, but he always did. She literally couldn't get it away from him. At the home visit, she told me that he would tire of it at some point and never want it again. That was his pattern with everything, including the food he ate. At any given period, he would only eat two of three foods.

I realized I had to try to solve the problem of Freddy by myself. I tried to teach Freddy the letters of the alphabet, but he was too busy flexing. I shocked him by slipping the straw out of his fingers and immediately offering it back by tapping it on the letter "A" and I said, "Here's the straw. Touch A! Touch A!" He reached for the straw and I "helped" his hand touch the card with the "A" on it and I said, "Good job! Letter A! Here's your straw". I let him flex it while I switched the cards and then I slipped it out of his fingers again! Again I held it on the letter "B" and said, "Touch B! Touch B!" He reached for the straw again and again I held his hand and tapped it on the card with the B while I said, "Good job! Letter B! Here's your straw." Without going through all 26 letters here, you can see what I did to start pairing his ability to flex that straw with his willingness to touch the card I asked him to touch. It took a few days, but he started touching the letters on his own and I began to be able to assess his skill level. It is so important to watch for clues while you work with your students. It reached the point that I loved that silly straw as much as Freddy did.

We went for about a month using the straw to work with Freddy and then one day he came to school without the straw. I had some others, but he didn't care one tiny bit about flexing the straw. My magic straw had lost all its power. What now? We struggled for a few days.

One morning, Freddy came with a box of Twinkies in his backpack with a note from his mother. It said, "Freddy is refusing to eat anything except Twinkies. If he won't eat lunch, please give him a Twinkie." We had a terrible morning because Freddy wanted a Twinkie. It hit me that I might be able to use the Twinkie the way I had used the straw. It worked. I went through reading, math, and writing groups with a half of one Twinkie as my bait. If he did the work, he got a tiny bite. It was enough. He didn't seem to care how much he got.

He was moving forward in academics at an amazing rate because, in fact, he was quite bright. He was definitely misplaced in a class for mentally handicapped children, but he certainly wouldn't have made it in a regular kindergarten at that point. I needed to be able to do something to get him to work without straws or Twinkies. It had to be something he was obsessing about because absolutely nothing else interested him. He didn't act like he even knew other children existed and only cared about me because I controlled the straws and Twinkies! I had to really think hard about this problem.

I had a language program in the classroom that used puppets. There also were some little plastic strips that had holes in them which could fit together into a long chain. I got an idea to use them to transition from a direct reward of the Twinkie mini bite to a plastic strip and when he gave me the strip, I quickly gave him a bite of Twinkie. Then, I made him perform two tasks, with the Twinkie right there in front of him with the plastic strips on top. When he had earned two strips I hooked them together and let him give them to me and I gave him a tiny bite. I kept this up until he was required to earn five strips to get one tiny bite. By transferring his reward to something a little more acceptable in a school classroom, I knew I was getting Freddy closer to a regular education placement. For a month I kept the Twinkie within his sight while he earned the plastic strips and the strips were kept on top of the Twinkie.

However, I knew I had to put the Twinkie out of sight. I started this phase by putting the Twinkie in a small container and the plastic strips on top of the container. I had to open the box many times before he earned the five strips in order to keep him aware of its location. I was literally praying that Freddy wouldn't lose his interest in Twinkies, but of course eventually he did. Imagine the thrill when I realized that Freddy started obsessing on the plastic strips.

I had several hundred plastic strips so I thought I had hit the jackpot. Freddy worked very fast in order to get more strips. It was great and I just loved the progress Freddy was making, but then I realized that we needed to get a bit closer to normal kindergarten reinforcement. I started a sticker card for Freddy. When he got his five plastic strips, he got a sticker on the card and the plastic strips went back into the main strip container. At first he didn't like that at all. I had to take it a little slower and I hung a little card with a sticker at the bottom of the strip. The stickers finally became the desired reward when I gave him the sticker first and when he got the next sticker, I let him put two strips together. When he got the next sticker, I let him put a third strip on the chain. Eventually, I was able to give him stickers only. When he filled the card with stickers, I allowed him to count the stickers and then count out that many plastic strips to string together into the chain. You can see that the reinforcement to get the skills learned must be as individualized as the skills.

At the end of that kindergarten year, we met with Freddy's parents, the school psychologist, and the general education primary program team leader to determine the best placement for Freddy for the next year. We decided to place him in the general education kindergarten. **Success**!

Summing It Up:

1. Children with autism are often unable to demonstrate their skill level. It is difficult but you need to find a way to assess his abilities.

2. If a child needs a special reinforcement or behavior plan, continue making modifications, if possible, to bring him or her more in line with typical plans so that he is able to handle the most typical classroom situation possible.

3. Remember that you are trying to help your students live in the "real world". You need to do what is necessary at the moment but always need to look ahead to see what their needs will be later.

4. Make the transition from a more restrictive plan to a less restrictive plan but if the steps are too big or too fast, the student may take a few steps backwards. Always keep an ongoing record of what is happening and be willing to modify your plan so the student will move forward.

Chapter 24:

Nancy

Sometimes I get down when I think of Nancy because I don't think I made a big enough difference in her behavior, but I managed some success, so I want to share her with you. She was 9 when she came to my class, but I had witnessed her fits since she was 5 in the primary program. She had cerebral palsy and had only a few words in her vocabulary.

At home, as I witnessed on home visits, she ruled the roost through intimidation and fear. One day when I was there, talking to her mom, Nancy slapped her sister's face very hard because her sister was sitting next to the mother. Her mother got up and got Nancy a cookie and turned on the TV for her. I saw many times that Nancy was actually rewarded for violence. Why shouldn't Nancy think violent behavior would also work at school? When she came to my class, she had been in school for four years and she still thought violence was the path to getting what she wanted, but it wasn't. Neither was picking up a table and throwing it when she wasn't chosen line leader, but that's further down in this story.

Nancy was incredibly strong and when she was having a tantrum her muscles seemed to lock in place. I don't know how such a little girl could be so strong, but she was. I was trained in how to safely restrain a person, how to protect myself from impending blows, and how to remove a hair puller's hands from a tangled fist full of hair without hurting the victim, but Nancy tested my physical strength to the absolute limit, and I still carry scars from my experience with her.

Above all else, I had to protect the other children in our class. It took less than a day to realize that I needed a separate aide just for Nancy, but it took almost a month to get one. That was a very difficult month.

We assigned jobs to each child in the classroom. We had a line leader, a calendar person, a door holder, and so on. There was a job for each of the 12 students in the classroom. To be fair, the jobs rotated. Nancy wanted all the jobs. All I had to say was, "It is time for our calendar person to come up and find our Monday card" and she would realize that she wasn't the calendar person. She would fly into action. It might be that she'd stand up and instantly attack the child who was the calendar person or she might jump up and push her desk over, but whatever she did, it was violent, sudden and extremely dangerous. She could move so quickly! I had to be sure my aide, Cynthia, stationed herself next to Nancy before I called on any child to do his job. We had to be between Nancy and the other children almost every minute, which made life in the classroom almost impossible.

During our academic time, the class was split into three groups of four. One group worked at individual desks, a second group worked with Cynthia and the third group worked with me. Nancy was seated right next to the teacher at the table. We rotated at the end of 20 minutes. She was always so happy when she was participating but she had absolutely **no** transition skills. To end an activity seemed like the end of the world to her. At first, when the time was up, I would say to the class, "Time to rotate" and Nancy would literally sweep our work table clean of everything. Pencils, papers, crayons, counters, whatever, went flying.

At the end of each group time, the students earned stickers for good behavior and she loved her stickers so **before** I announced that we needed to rotate to the new group, I let her choose which sticker she wanted and then cleared most of the other items from the table while she selected. It helped a little, but we still had problems. I knew that once she got to Cynthia's group she would be cooperative and happy until she had to change again, so I added a special sticker card she took to Cynthia's table where Nancy received a sticker as soon as she sat down. That worked really well as long as we stayed in a state of hyper-vigilance.

Nancy's lack of language played a huge role in her behavior so we worked on signing and picture communication boards. They helped as long as we could predict quickly enough what would send her into attack mode. By involving her to some degree, we made some progress. For example, we showed her a card with each student's picture on it and asked her to show us the calendar person and she would point out the person. That seemed to diffuse her frustration to some degree.

Once I was given a 1:1 aide for Nancy, I set up a strict behavior plan. Amanda, her aide, stayed right with her, but if Nancy was violent toward anyone she was removed and placed in a timeout room in a corner of my classroom. Once her tantrum stopped, she was brought back to the group. For the rest of that school year, we continued making some progress but it was slow. She still had to be handled very carefully during each transition and during each of the times when another child needed to perform his classroom job. My hardest task was to give the other 11 children a school experience that was free of fear, but I knew I wasn't succeeding. They were very leery of her.

Amanda was wonderful and 100% consistent. I knew how much of a physical strain it was on her to get Nancy to the timeout room and many times it required two of us to get her there. I was afraid she'd quit the job but she didn't.

At the beginning of the second year with Nancy, the three of us met and went over the exact plan for Nancy. We used the communication board and, the timeout procedure for violence against others, and we also thought of a few other positive ideas for ways to involve Nancy with other children in an appropriate way. We planned some activities in which we paired the students in a cooperative "taking turns" game.

I met with Nancy's mom at the home visit and made several suggestions about trying to deal with Nancy's violence at home. I knew I was in trouble when her mother told me that Nancy wasn't violent at home. About two minutes after that comment was made, Nancy pushed her sister out of the chair she was in and kicked her. Her mother ignored it. I asked her how she generally handled that type of action and she said that she usually just let the girls fight it out. I didn't feel too hopeful when I left that home visit.

We all noticed how much Nancy had grown over that summer. She was now almost 11 and even stronger than before. The funny thing was that she absolutely loved school, but she just wanted everything to go her way. After awhile, though, with the timeout program combined with the stickers for every 15 minutes she stayed out of that room, she did start to improve, but she was still throwing tantrums and hurting the furniture and supplies, so I decided to upgrade the timeout program to include violence to people and equipment. We tried to prevent any problems before they could happen but it didn't always work. She was very unpredictable.

I believe in positive reinforcement and have a very strong belief in the natural desire of every child to be good and I believed it of Nancy, too, but her quick violence presented too great a danger to others and to the environment. Because she went into the timeout room more often, she became angrier. I had to come up with something better, but what?

Our lives that year reached a perfect storm one week in January. Another child in the class had become upset and had unintentionally broken Cynthia's arm when he struck out, so she was in a cast. She was trying to control another boy and Amanda assisted her. The boy scratched the back of Amanda's hand and it became infected. She had a big bandage on it, but she was trying to finish out the day with Nancy. I didn't want her hurt further, so when we came up to the classroom after lunch recess and our door holder stepped forward to open the door and, Nancy lunged at him, I stopped her and started toward the timeout area. However, she fought so hard that I had to restrain her and injured both of my wrists. I sent Cynthia to the office for help. They called Nancy's mother, who took 45 minutes to get to the school, even though she lived about five minutes away. I was still restraining Nancy when she came in the door. Nancy ran to her mother to be hugged, and sadly, she got that hug.

This scene I've described was the low point of my teaching career. I really felt discouraged. There we were. One of my aides had a broken arm, the other a bandaged hand, and I could barely move my hands because my wrists were completely strained. But the children were fantastic. We had a good afternoon with them, but as soon as the buses left that day, I walked into my principal's office and burst into tears and said, "I have absolutely *no* idea how we will possibly handle Nancy tomorrow."

My principal, who had been a special education teacher, was extremely supportive of my program. She immediately looked up Nancy's home phone number, called her mother, and said, "Nancy is suspended until all three members of the staff are completely healed." She also called for a meeting with the district's head of special education. When we met he told me that I had tried everything I could, but I had waited too long to get support from him. I know he was right, but it just never occurred to me to give up on any child.

For the rest of that school year, our district paid a private facility to educate Nancy. She was placed in a program with two other students and four adults. The teacher of that class called me several times and indicated that Nancy had made very little progress. The next year, the district brought her back to our district's program for severe behavioral and emotionally handicapped students. She was in a class by herself with a teacher and an aide. I was dumbfounded and really sad.

Several years later, I was at a Special Olympics event and I saw Nancy and her mother. Nancy was a grown woman but she recognized me immediately. She was in a wheelchair by then, but when I walked over to her, she beamed and gave me a huge hug. I hugged her back and felt it was my apology for not helping her as I wanted to.

Summing It Up:

1. Try as hard as you can to succeed with each child. If you need help from district authorities, ask for it.
2. Develop a plan and be consistent.
3. Keep excellent data on any behavior plan. If it is something as drastic as timeout, be sure you follow all guidelines of your school or district.
4. Do whatever you have to do to keep the other children in your classroom safe.

Chapter 25:

Barry

I have saved my crowning achievement for the last chapter. Barry was one of the most difficult children I taught during my 40-year career and he was my greatest success. He vindicated my decision to become a teacher and demonstrated what I have been emphasizing in this book. He reinforced my belief that every child is worth our very best, most creative effort; every child, no matter how unlovable, deserves our love; every child *can* change and become acceptable without sacrificing the uniqueness of his personality, and every child can learn. It's all up to us.

Barry was 7 when he came to my class of intermediate moderately mentally handicapped students. All of my other students were between 9 and 12. The district called me after about a month of school to tell me they were sending him to me because he was so unruly that he was injuring the primary students in his current class. He was big and strong and very aggressive. I got a call from his teacher that day telling me that she had tried for two years and he was "not teachable, was mean, and irritating, and had made zero progress in two years." I was speechless to hear a teacher talk that way.

I actually heard Barry coming down the wide hallway outside of our classroom on his first day with us because he literally bounced from wall to wall while he clapped, jumped, ran, and whooped all the way. A district administrator brought him to me---that was a first. He ran to the toy shelf, grabbed one of those little wooden Fisher Price people and bit the head off! It was recess time so out we went and I was happy that Barry stayed on the playground. He was excited about our big climbing apparatus which kept him engaged and he didn't hurt anyone. He was so happy and playing so well that I couldn't imagine he deserved his bad reputation. When we lined up, he ran up to me and started slapping his jean's pocket and said, "Barb, do you want a joint?"

"No, thank you Barry," I replied, taking his hand, and we walked together into the classroom to begin five years of working toward civilization.

I had Barry in my class longer than any other child I taught. Usually, I had a student through his intermediate grades (fourth, fifth, and sixth), but since he was assigned to me when he was a second grader, our time together was longer. The truth is, though, that I needed all five years.

Barry contracted spinal meningitis in infancy, causing mental delays. He was extremely hyperactive, but when his doctor prescribed drugs for hyperactivity, it made Barry much more active. He had to be taken off of those drugs and was never on them again. He was very strong with no idea of his strength. All parts of his body were strong, including his teeth. Just a hug from Barry could break a rib.

He was easily frustrated and reacted to his frustration by slamming his left fist in his mouth and striking horizontally with his right arm. He wasn't trying to hit anyone, but if anyone happened to be standing on Barry's right side when he got frustrated, watch out! He had a normal vocabulary for his age but added to that, unfortunately, was all of the profanity imaginable. He smiled from ear to ear and found a lot in life to be very funny. He had a spectacular laugh, although in assemblies our principal wasn't too thrilled with the volume. He was just about as inappropriate a child as you can imagine, but a wonderful boy full of vim and vigor.

Barry had a shock of black hair that stood straight on end. It always needed cutting. His brown eyes were huge, filled with anticipation. He exuded excitement. Although he was only 7, he was as tall as my 9 year olds, and huskier than any of them. He was distracted by **everything** he saw, and he saw everything.

Barry's family was interesting. His father had been incarcerated for most of Barry's life and his mother loved to ride motorcycles and get tattoos. She struggled financially. Barry was her only child and she adored him but she didn't understand calm, consistent discipline and limit-setting. Her sister and her niece lived with them and they were also adorned with many tattoos.

One day we were on the playground when Barry's aunt came roaring up on a loud motorcycle to pick him up early from school. She walked up to us and said to Barry, "Hey Butthead, are ya ready to go?" Then she goosed Barry, who immediately goosed her back! Both of them were howling with laughter. It was so inappropriate that I was dumbfounded.

"Barry, you can't do that to anyone, especially a girl," I said. I could understand Barry's look of surprise, but when his aunt had the same look on her face, I was flabbergasted. I asked Barry to go with Cynthia, my aide, to get his backpack from the classroom. After he was out of earshot, I tried to explain that it might be better not to use terms of "endearment" such as "Butthead" with him since that type of language was getting him into trouble at school. She didn't get it at all. I had so much work to do and only five years to do it.

At the time Barry came to my class, I had eight other students and one aide, Cynthia. It took only minutes to figure out huge changes must occur. There simply was no way to teach Barry in our academic group time. My aide and I each had four in a group for 20 minutes, although we taught each child independently. While we worked with one, we had a worksheet or book for the other children. Barry destroyed almost everything he touched. He ripped the cover off of a book the second it got into his hands. He tore the worksheets. He took the crayon I gave him, instantly put it under the leg of his chair, lifted up the chair, and came down on the crayon, grinding it into the carpet. Nothing could be on the table in front of him.

Although he had been in school for two years, he had no appropriate school behaviors. At the end of that first day, I told Cynthia that I would work out a total change in the room arrangement and routine. The first step was to teach Barry how to be a student.

I checked with our custodian, a very important person to know at the school, and commandeered a privacy cubby to set up a learning station for Barry. The high walls on three sides made it impossible for him to see anyone else in the room. It had a work table attached and two chairs, one for him and one for the teacher. Right in front of the cubby, I put a 48-inch rectangular table with two chairs side by side. On the other side of the classroom, I put four desks on one side of a small work table. The work table had four student chairs and a teacher's chair.

When it was time for the first academic group time, I took Barry to his work cubby and Cynthia took her first group of four students to the table. The other four students went to the four desks and had an independent activity to do while they waited for their turn with Cynthia. At the end of the 20 minutes, we rotated. Barry and I sat at the table in front of his cubby and the aide sent her four students to the desks and the desk students came to her table to work on reading, math, or writing. Each day, I switched positions with Cynthia so that we wouldn't be too exhausted from working with Barry.

In order to keep Barry's attention, I discovered that if I acted more hyper than he did, he calmed down and watched me with a big smile on his face. It worked! He loved my car, which was a Volkswagen bug I called Pipsqueak, so I often drew a big picture of my car, bit by bit, as he responded to what I was asking him to do, academically. For example, I'd say in a fast, excited way, "Hey, Barry, do you want a picture of Pipsqueak?" while drawing the main car shape. Then I'd put out three letter cards, A, B, and C and say, "Touch A, Barry! Touch A and I'll draw the wheel. Hurry, Barry! Touch A!" After he touched the letter, I'd draw one wheel very quickly and then say, "Touch B! Barry, touch B! We need another wheel, Hurry, Hurry, Touch B!" and he would. We drew constantly in between each part of the lesson. By the end of the 20 minutes, I would be completely exhausted and he would be happy and quite calm. It was truly astounding how it worked. When the timer rang, it meant it was time to rotate. I also needed to teach him to calmly get up and walk to his next station.

To teach Barry to work independently, I placed one item on the table. He learned to sit and put his hands in his lap and then to work with the item. I had one crayon and a coloring page (to color not to crush, tear, or throw), or I had three small blocks to stack (to stack, not to throw or bite), or I had a very simple three piece puzzle (to insert the pieces, not to throw, or bang on the table). There was a lot more to this whole process and it took a very long time before Barry started to understand the routine. Eventually, I put two of the items on the table and after his hands were in his lap, I told him to get the crayon and paper to work with. He learned to leave the other item alone unless asked to get it. It was almost the whole school year before we got to that point.

Other than the academic period, which was an hour before recess and an hour after recess, Barry was with the class. Our problems never stopped wherever he was. At recess, he pushed students off the equipment, he urinated on the grass, he swore using the dreaded "F" word, and he refused to line up. During our free time in the classroom in the afternoon, he was so hard on the equipment that he broke toys and machines.

We had a record player and his first choice each day was to play records. No teacher in her right mind had ever let him near the record player, but I decided to use it to teach him to be careful with supplies. As I've mentioned in other chapters, we always have faster success if we use what the student is truly interested in. It is just common sense, but record players don't come cheap! I held his hand and stroked the back of it telling him how gentle he had to be when he put the needle onto the record. I helped him do it several times and then let him try alone. He was shaking with happiness. I mean that. He was shaking with joy. No one had ever entrusted him with the record player. He scratched many a record, but it wasn't too serious and he was feeling so great!

Toward the end of free time that first day that he used the record player, I made a big mistake. Barry was happily playing records while another little boy was busy stacking blocks about five feet away. I had walked across the room when I realized playtime was over and we needed to clean up pretty quickly to get ready to go home. My error was saying, from that distance, "Time to clean up".

Barry screamed, "NO!" as he whirled around and kicked the other student in the back. I honestly thought he killed him! I told Cynthia to get the child to the nurse.

I walked over to Barry and said, "Barry, do you still want to play the records?" I could read his mind. He thought this was his one and only chance to play the record player and he was frantic. "Show me how gently you put the needle on that record. I want to see how well you do it." He calmed right down and put the needle on. "Tomorrow during free time, **you** get the record player again. Now, when I say, "Time to clean up", will you show me how gently you take the needle off and how you can take that record off, too?" I was so worried about Mike, the injured child, but it was critical that Barry learn how to stop playing without such anxiety that he struck out. Once he realized that we were actually going to let him use the equipment that any of the other children could use, he never had a problem when it was time to clean up. Mike was fine, thank goodness.

When Cynthia brought Mike back to the room, Barry ran to him, hugged him painfully, kissed him and said, "Shit, man! I'm sorry I kicked you!" Oh well, I let that one slide.

Every Thursday we took our class into the community, as I have mentioned, to participate in a community leisure activity and then we had lunch and went grocery shopping. Each student worked on the grocery shopping skills at his level. At the beginning, we had to be sure Barry knew how to push the grocery cart safely. He didn't. I was walking up and down each aisle with him while he pushed the cart but suddenly he began to run with it and then jumped onto the back and sailed down the aisle, jumped off and laid it on its side while he made "vroom" motorcycle noises. We had a very long road ahead of us at the grocery store.

Swearing was always an issue with Barry and it really was a severe problem in the community. We had a rule that if he swore, my aide took him back to the van and he was banned from activity for a certain amount of time. That worked quite well, but it usually involved a tantrum before he calmed down. In the classroom, he was taken out into the hall for a few minutes before he could return. Eventually, the swearing decreased dramatically. He didn't like to miss out on anything.

At the end of the first year, Barry was still working behind the privacy cubby and at his independent work table with either Cynthia or me. He had progressed in school behaviors as well as academic skills. He was working in a reading program and doing basic math pre-requisite skills such as counting and numerals, and he was able to print his first name.

When the second year began, he wasn't at school on the first day, or the second. I called his house and the phone was disconnected. On the third day he was brought to school by a Child Protective Service worker who told me he had been placed in a foster home temporarily. He was there for about five disastrous months. I went to the foster home for my home visit that fall and felt uneasy. His foster mother, Ellen, was quite timid and his foster father was overbearing and couldn't feel any compassion for Barry. His attitude was "these are the rules and he has to obey." Of course, I believed Barry did need rules, but he also needed kindness and acceptance and I wasn't seeing any of that. Over the next three months, Barry continued to love school but he swore more and seemed much more frustrated. He talked about his mom and kept asking to go home. His mother was in jail for six months, but I don't think Barry ever knew that. He just knew he wasn't able to go home.

Occasionally, he said something that concerned me, such as "Bob [the foster father] broke my gun." A call to the foster home told me that Barry was using a stick, pretending it was a gun. When Bob heard him "shooting", he took it from Barry and snapped it in half. Bob always seemed to correct Barry in an angry way, which didn't help Barry at all to become a calm, sensible person. I was getting quite concerned so I called the case manager to talk about it with her. She said they were so short on homes to take the harder children, and she hadn't seen any signs of abuse from Bob, so she thought everything was okay. She knew Bob was quite strict, but she felt that he needed to be. I had to let my concern go for then.

After Christmas break, Barry came back to school very excited because he had gotten a new bike for Christmas from Bob and Ellen. A week later, he came to school in a foul mood. Evidently, Bob had broken Barry's bike. I couldn't get Barry past this, so I called to have another home visit with Bob and Ellen. I asked about the broken bike and Bob told me the story. He had been trying to get Barry to put the bike away properly each evening but Barry just left it on the sideway or in the yard. Bob's punishment was to get a sledge hammer and beat the bike's spokes out and basically destroy the bicycle, in front of Barry. I was beside myself. Such a demonstration of angry violence was the very last thing this child needed. I tried to explain that to Bob who didn't want to listen at all. I called the case worker again, and Barry was removed from that home. He was back with his mother in the spring of that second year. She had problems, but she loved him and tried her best.

We learned quickly that we needed to walk next to Barry on his left side because if he was frustrated or angry, his immediate reaction was to suddenly bite his left fist and swing out horizontally with his right hand. This happened when we denied him something or if he perceived that he might be denied or removed. One day, during free time, he wanted a toy belonging to another child, who wasn't willing to give it up. Barry said, "F- - -you!"

Cynthia said, "Let's go, Barry" and he knew that meant outside of the classroom for five minutes. By this point, he usually went out with her, swearing all the way. She made the mistake of walking on his right side and when he bit his fist and flailed out with his right, he basically karate chopped her arm and broke it.

When she showed up the next day with a cast, he was devastated. He never meant to hurt anyone. Cynthia was very upset, and her husband almost forced her to resign, but thank goodness she didn't. She knew the miracles we had worked together, but she said, "I just don't know if he belongs here. I don't think we're going to make it with Barry." I was afraid she might be right, but I told her that if I felt that way, I might as well resign. We had to succeed with all of our students. Failure was not an option. I couldn't give up on him. He just reacted so fast without thinking.

It took us another two years to see him exercise self-control during frustration or anger. In the meantime, no one walked on his right side again.

During the third year with Barry, I was able to integrate him into the academic groups. I made his group the smaller one, with just three children in it. The other two children in his group had the best independent skills in our class, so all 3 were able to learn. It had taken a little over two years to get to this point where Barry understood to keep his hands to himself, treat materials with respect, never touch items belonging to others, and be able to do something constructive (coloring, a puzzle, look at a book)while I worked with the other children. We still had moments of course, but he was succeeding. He was also growing. He was going to be a very large, tall man and at age 9 he was the largest child in our classroom of 9 to 12-year-olds. Finally, he had reached the actual age of the students in the intermediate program.

Everyone at our elementary school knew Barry, primarily because of his foul mouth. He was still very loud and his swearing had diminished but when it occurred, it was wild. We kept very good records of his behavior program. We recorded each time he swore, hit, hurt property, or failed to line up, which was still a big problem in the third year. Working with 12 handicapped children made recording cumbersome. We were recording data for all 12. Some were easy because the occurrence was less frequent, but we needed a quick way to keep accurate records that could be put on the charts at the end of the day.

We always wore pants to work because we had to be on the floor, climbing playground equipment to retrieve kids, and so on, so we put strips of masking tape on our pant legs with the child's initial and a behavior. For example, a strip would have "B hit." Another strip below that one would say "B Swear." We made a quick hash mark for each time he hit or swore during the day. It was a simple way to keep accurate records. Sometimes we looked like zebras with all those stripes! At the end of each day, I combined our tape data onto behavior charts. When you keep good data, and make charts to show progress or lack of progress, you will find that you stay on top of the situation and can modify what you are doing to improve your results. We had data covering five years by the time Barry left us for the junior high program.

In our fourth year with Barry, I wrote in my weekly newsletter to the parents, that Barry was the most improved student I had ever taught. He was now shopping independently for four items at the grocery store, and was pushing the grocery cart carefully. We did have one funny incident with his cart that year. He was at one end of the aisle and I was watching him from the other end. He had his item but couldn't keep coming down the aisle because there were so many people and carts in it. He waited very patiently, but he had only so much patience. Finally, he yelled, "HEY, I HAVE TO GET TO **HER**!" The people parted like the Red Sea, and he continued down the aisle sporting that beautiful beaming smile. I was the most proud that day because he didn't swear at those shoppers.

By the end of the fourth year, we heard less swearing, but it still occurred. One day we had an assembly in which a dignitary was speaking about Arizona history. The whole school was excited about the event and Barry was no exception. Before we went in for the presentation, I talked to him about appropriate manners. He got this same pep talk before we went into any social setting. He knew that he would be removed if he swore. After the presentation, the principal asked the student body if anyone had a question for the speaker. Barry raised his hand very enthusiastically. Mrs. James, the principal, saw him but I could tell she was afraid to call on him for fear of what he might say. Truly, there was no telling what he might say, so I couldn't really blame her. Child after child was called on, but not Barry. Finally, he screamed, "YOU BUTTFACE! DON'T YOU SEE MY HAND?" Oh dear, out I went with a very frustrated Barry-and yes, I walked on his left side. When the assembly was over, and he had calmed down, I told him that I wanted him to go in and apologize to Mrs. James for the rude comment. When we started down the auditorium's central aisle, Mrs. James was talking to the speaker. Barry took off at a run and literally threw himself at the speaker, gave her one of those wild Barry hugs and said, "I LOVE YOU!" We were all so surprised, but it was so genuine. I asked him to apologize to Mrs. James for the comment and he gave her a big hug and apologized. You just couldn't stay angry with a boy with so much love in him.

At the end of our fifth year with Barry, Cynthia and I felt like we were giving up a child of our own. At the end of the year, I asked Barry about his summer plans. He told me, "My mom said I can get a tattoo!" He probably did end up with many tattoos. We had been through so many wild times with him and had witnessed a completely uncivilized terror of a 7-year-old become a very nice, generally well-behaved young man of 12. At the sixth grade graduation ceremonies that May, we all got those bear hugs from him and I saw tears on many faces. Everyone at our school knew him and appreciated his accomplishments. We saw him many times over the next few years and knew that he would be just fine.

Summing It Up:

1. Do not judge a child totally by the previous teacher's comments. I never looked at the behavior records of my students before meeting them.

2. If you teach special education, you will know a lot about your students before you see them because of the required placement meetings, but if you hear a lot of negative comments, try your best to give the child a fresh start and meet him and his needs with an open mind.

3. Analyze what the student needs in order to succeed.

4. Give him a chance to prove himself. Structure situations to ensure safety for all the students.

5. Keep good records including for behavior goals.

6. Become good friends with the custodian. He knows where all the extra furniture is.